"An invitation to reflect on what it means that God became *human*. . . . Here is a resource to invite multisensory engagement at this sacred time of year, to slow down and fully experience the mystery of God's presence in human form—Jesus—and the mystery of God's presence in us."

—**Mandy Smith**, pastor and author

"Amanda and Hannah have written the rare book where the ordinary and extraordinary intersect in the most believable and poignant ways. I recommend *Sense of Wonder* for your journey of faith through the holidays."

—**Shane Stanford**, author and former United Methodist pastor of 30 years, and current president of JourneyWise, a faith-based multimedia ministry

"There is a lot of focus on how to connect with God through knowledge, with our 'minds,' but less focus on how to connect with God with our bodies, hearts, and souls. And yet Jesus says that to love him, we must use all of these senses (Luke 10:27). *Sense of Wonder* invites you to bring yourself, fully embodied, into your relationship with Christ this holiday season."

—**Heather Thompson Day**, author of *I'll See You Tomorrow*

SENSE OF WONDER

Delighting in
God's Presence
throughout the
HOLIDAY SEASON

Hannah Opliger & Amanda Luedeke

Our Daily Bread
Publishing.

Requests for permission to quote from this book should be directed to: Permissions Department, Our Daily Bread Publishing, PO Box 3566, Grand Rapids, MI 49501, or contact us by email at permissionsdept@odb.org.

Scripture quotations, unless otherwise indicated, are taken from the Holy Bible, New International Version®, NIV®. Copyright © 1973, 1978, 1984, 2011 by Biblica, Inc.™ Used by permission of Zondervan. All rights reserved worldwide. www.zondervan.com.
    Scripture quotations marked ESV are taken from the ESV® Bible (The Holy Bible, English Standard Version®), copyright © 2001 by Crossway, a publishing ministry of Good News Publishers. Used by permission. All rights reserved.
    Scripture quotations marked ISV are taken from the Holy Bible: International Standard Version®. Copyright © 1995–2014 by ISV Foundation. ALL RIGHTS RESERVED INTERNATIONALLY. Used by permission of Davidson Press, LLC.
    Scripture quotations marked NET are taken from the NET Bible®, copyright © 1996, 2019 by Biblical Studies Press, L.L.C. All rights reserved. Scripture quoted by permission. http://netbible.com.
    Scripture quotations marked NKJV are taken from the New King James Version®. Copyright © 1982 by Thomas Nelson. Used by permission. All rights reserved.

Interior design by Michael J. Williams

Library of Congress Cataloging-in-Publication Data

Names: Opliger, Hannah, author. | Luedeke, Amanda, author.
Title: Sense of wonder : delighting in God's presence throughout the holiday season / Hannah Opliger & Amanda Luedeke.
Description: Grand Rapids, MI : Our Daily Bread Publishing, [2024] | Summary: "50 devotions guide readers on a multisensory holiday experience from Thanksgiving to New Year's Day. As readers anticipate the arrival of God in human flesh, they engage His presence with all 5 senses and their whole selves"-- Provided by publisher.
Identifiers: LCCN 2023055952 (print) | LCCN 2023055953 (ebook) | ISBN 9781640703391 (paperback) | ISBN 9781640703407 (epub)
Subjects: LCSH: Christmas. | Holidays--Religious aspects--Christianity.
Classification: LCC BV45 .O657 2024 (print) | LCC BV45 (ebook) | DDC 242/.33--dc23/eng/20240125
LC record available at https://lccn.loc.gov/2023055952
LC ebook record available at https://lccn.loc.gov/2023055953

Printed in Europe
24 25 26 27 28 29 30 31 / 8 7 6 5 4 3 2 1

We dedicate this book to
the brothers and sisters of Northeast Church in Fort Wayne,
who have been the landscape for us to grow and be formed,
to mess up, to be vulnerable,
and to courageously use our gifts.
Let's keep living the Beautiful Way of Jesus together.

CONTENTS

INTRODUCTION

The holiday season, in many ways, has been hijacked. Instead of earth receiving her King, she seems to get stressed out and bent on consumerism. We look forward to this time with nostalgia, and then, somewhere in the midst of it all, we realize that we're worn-out, overcommitted, frantic, and not at all the people we want to be during a meaningful season. The holidays become a fast-moving six-or-so-week sprint that leaves us weary and longing for more meaning—and then glad it's over.

At this time of year, maybe more than any other time, even though the calendar may be full, we tend to disconnect from others, from God, and even from parts of ourselves. For some, this disconnection happens when our focus is on the things we need to do. Life becomes a checklist, full of holiday planning and travel and end-of-the-year business reports and deliverables. For others, this disconnection happens when our focus is so inward that all we can see is our own desires, longings, and year-end what-ifs.

Disconnection wreaks havoc in every aspect of our lives. We cannot flourish without being connected to God, others, and ourselves—it's how we were made.

How do we change this? How do we reconnect and fully experience all that is before us this holiday season?

Human Beings with Human Needs

God created us with bodies and said it was very good. Jesus came and dwelled among us in a body. He resurrected back to life after death in His body. So we, too, include our bodies in our seeking of Jesus and in our spiritual formation. We don't just have bodies; we are bodies. Bodily creatures.

And of course these bodies come with all sorts of needs. To thrive as bodies, we need connection to God, ourselves, and others. This holiday season of Thanksgiving (in the United States), Christmas, and the New Year is no different. When the holidays get busy and we begin to mentally and even physically disconnect, we miss out on the quiet but steady invitation from God to pause. He invites us to see, touch, hear, smell, taste, and sense that He is with us and at work, for our relationships with God are not one-dimensional.

And *that* is the hope of this devotional.

In the uniqueness of the season, this book creates space to engage God's presence with our whole selves, including our senses and emotions, as we believe intimacy with Him is meant to be full, multisensory, and experiential.

He created us to *see* Him in nature and the people around us.
He created us to *feel* His presence in the wind, the rain, and a walk in the woods.
He created us to *hear* Him in a children's choir, in birdsong, and in a quiet whisper.
He created us to *smell* His creativity in the scent of Christmas pine and Grandma's from-scratch sugar cookies.
He created us to *taste* His faithful provision in the warmth of our morning coffee and in the sharing of bread and wine at the Lord's Table.
He created us to *experience* self-awareness as we're also aware of His presence.

The Sixth Sense

You may be curious about the last sense we mentioned—the one we're calling *self-awareness*. While the other senses are self-explanatory, this sixth sense is worthy of elaboration.

The term *proprioception* was first coined in 1906 by Charles Scott Sherrington, a neurophysiologist. The word comes from the Latin *propriu*, which means "one's own," and *percepio*, which means "perceive." This term describes the gathering of sensory information from microscopic neural receptors embedded in joints, muscles, and tendons that allows a person to sense where their physical body is at any given moment, in any location. Sherrington defined it as "the perception of joints and body movement as well as position of the body, or body segments, in space."[1]

In essence, Sherrington had identified a sixth sense.

Today, there is heightened attention given to this sense as researchers try to understand proprioceptive dysfunction, especially in children. "Children suffering from proprioceptive dysfunction are uncoordinated and have difficulty performing basic normal childhood tasks and activities. They don't experience the world like the majority of people."[2]

While research on proprioception centers around brain and body physiology, we know that our emotions, our thoughts, our convictions, our desires are intrinsically intertwined with our body's experience of the world. As Tish Harrison Warren puts it, "Christianity is a thoroughly embodied faith. We believe in the incarnation—Christ came in a body. . . . In the Scriptures we find that the body is not incidental to our faith, but integral to our worship."[3] This time of year, more than any other time, we remember and rejoice that God came to redeem humanity through humanity, in the person of Jesus.

This sixth sense—our ability to perceive in our bodies our very existence in time and space—is about our whole-self experience of the world. Proprioception is a mouthful, so for the sake of this book, we'll refer to it as *self-awareness*. Self-awareness is the sense we probably rely on the most *while also* ignoring it the most. For that reason, we have included more opportunities to practice self-awareness than any other sense in the devotional.

Like Jesus, we are in this moment in a body. We take up space. We are present. We have feelings in our body and in our mind in real time. And thanks be to God, Jesus wants to meet us not in ignoring our self but in being self-aware. Let's practice that together.

How to Use This Book

We want it to be as simple and natural as possible for you to engage your senses as you read this book. Each entry begins with an opportunity to prepare. You will notice a symbol beside these prepare sections, indicating which of the six senses we are asking you to pay attention to.

The prepare exercise gives you the mindset and space to focus on one bodily sense in the presence of God before you turn to His Word. Even if you aren't able to do the suggested exercise, using your imagination to picture yourself doing the activity will help you include that part of your brain. The hope is that God would use the prepare exercise to help you be more fully present and available to God.

From there you will be given a Scripture passage to partake of, a short devotion to ponder, a prayer to read, and an activity to practice. The practice section provides some daily-life ways to take the devotion further, making it more fruitful. It's a way to allow what you're thinking about to spill out into everyday life and your interactions with others.

Some of the prepare and practice sections throughout the book invite you to consider and name what you're feeling, your emotions. For some of us, this can feel like uncharted territory. Perhaps identifying what you're feeling is difficult, much less putting words to your emotions. You are not alone. For these sections, it's helpful to get as specific as you can. Try to venture beyond the primary emotions of happiness, sadness, fear, and anger. Ask yourself, "What is underneath this feeling I have? What's the feeling beneath the feeling?" Googling a "feelings wheel" can help with increasing your emotional vocabulary and imagination.

Practically speaking, we've provided enough content so you can read an entry every day from the week of Thanksgiving (in the United States) through the New Year. Regardless of which day of the month Thanksgiving is this year, if you want to use all seven weeks of devotions in this book, you will start reading on November 20 and end on January 7.

But that isn't the only way to meet with God using this book. This devotional lends itself to being picked up and leafed through at any time during the holidays. The entries all stand alone and the order isn't mandatory, though in some ways they do build on one another. But we recognize that we each have unique needs at this time of year, and this devotional has space for that. It's here for you, whether you use it only a few times every holiday season or engage the full book year after year.

Our Prayer for You

We believe King Jesus wants to meet you in all your human vulnerability. We believe He wants to show you His glory this holiday season. What better way to meet Jesus, the Son of Man, than to encounter His presence with all your very human senses? To pray and seek God with both the head *and* the heart? To love the Lord your God with *all* your heart, soul, mind, and strength? To reclaim the holidays for your heart's formation and the glory of God?

With this posture and using this daily practice, let's experience the wonder of God together.

Hannah & Amanda

PREPARING
FOR THE KING

On the American calendar, gratitude is always at the start of the holiday season. Before the Christmas festivities, before the gift giving, before the family gatherings, school's winter break, and time off work, we feast with thanksgiving. We sit around a table and, with varying levels of intentionality, we give thanks.

There is beauty in this—and if we're honest, there's power in it too.

In an individualized consumer culture that has lost touch with the art of true thankfulness, Thanksgiving is an opportunity for us to rewrite the script. To pause and check our hearts. To make space for greater awareness of God's goodness. To receive Him in the places where He has been present all along.

Jesus invites us to a life of gratitude. He asks us to cease striving and to lay down heavy loads we aren't meant to carry. He's inviting us to a new way of seeing, feeling, hearing, smelling, tasting, and being self-aware in the world around us as we experience *His presence in it*. To really notice and give thanks.

This Thanksgiving section offers seven simple devotions. Read one, read all—you get to choose. Just pay attention to how the Lord may be inviting you into something deeper with Him this Thanksgiving.

SATISFACTION IN THE SMALL THINGS

Play a song that always brought you joy and excitement as a child, or perhaps a song that was on repeat during your high school or college years. Notice how the song makes you feel. Notice how something so simple can have such a strong impact.

"As surely as the LORD your God lives," she replied, "I don't have any bread—only a handful of flour in a jar and a little olive oil in a jug. I am gathering a few sticks to take home and make a meal for myself and my son, that we may eat it—and die."

Elijah said to her, "Don't be afraid. Go home and do as you have said. But first make a small loaf of bread for me from what you have and bring it to me, and then make something for yourself and your son. For this is what the LORD, the God of Israel, says: 'The jar of flour will not be used up and the jug of oil will not run dry until the day the LORD sends rain on the land.'"

She went away and did as Elijah had told her. So there was food every day for Elijah and for the woman and her family. For the jar of flour was not used up and the jug of oil did not run dry, in keeping with the word of the LORD spoken by Elijah.

1 Kings 17:12–16

When I envision the perfect holiday season, it always looks like this: My house is spotless, with tasteful decorations drawing people in to the festivities. Our calendar is filled to the brim with meaningful gatherings, and all my favorite people are able to attend. There's margin for rest and recuperation. My children are well-behaved, and they thank me endlessly for my efforts.

Yet reality rarely lives up to the fantasy I've created in my mind. My "perfect Thanksgiving" never happens the way I plan, yet I continue to enjoy and have wonderful memories of the holiday.

When you think of your favorite Thanksgiving memories, what comes to mind?

As you look at your list, you might notice it's made up of many small, simple, and unplanned moments rather than big, flashy Thanksgiving memories. It's the smell of Grandma's pie. Your uncle telling the same childhood story dozens of times. You've heard it year after year and yet not often enough. It's the unexpected handmade gift from a dear friend. The feeling of joy while catching up with cousins you haven't seen in ages. The anticipation of getting out the Christmas decorations and turning your attention to what's still to come.

These are the things, the moments, we carry with us for the rest of our lives. They are what make the holidays so special.

It's the seemingly insignificant things that have the biggest impact. Look at the story in 1 Kings 17. The widow at Zarephath had next to nothing when Elijah visited her. Yet the simple, seemingly insignificant act of baking him bread jump-started a season of renewal for her. She and her family were saved from starvation, and later in the chapter Elijah brought her son back to life (vv. 17–24).

The small act of obeying God and baking bread led to incredible miracles for that family!

What's another example from the Bible of a seemingly insignificant moment that brought about great change? (Consider Ruth's decision to stay with Naomi in Ruth 1 or Joseph's willingness to interpret the dreams of prisoners in Genesis 40.)

The Bible reminds us again and again that there is power in the small and insignificant. Let's remember that when our expectations for the season begin to cloud our ability to enjoy and be faithful in the moments before us.

My Jesus, You came to this world—quietly, meekly, yet beautifully—and changed everything. I thank You and praise You for showing us that power isn't found only in what is big and flashy. Help me to cling to this! Help me to focus on the importance of a smile. Kindness to a stranger. A heartfelt invitation to reconnect with others. Guide me away from the big efforts that impress and replace that desire with an ability to see Your work in the small things.

Today, when you feel pressured to produce a certain holiday experience for others, take a step back. Reflect on your list of Thanksgiving memories and consider how you might shift your expectations to make room for what may seem insignificant.

FILLED TO FORGETFULNESS

 Making a gratitude list is becoming quite a validated practice—for those both within and outside of the church. In preparation for today's entry, make a gratitude list using the sense of smell. (For instance, I'm thankful for the smell of freshly cut grass after the accomplishment of mowing. Or I'm thankful for the smell of soup when we're welcomed into our friends' home and get to receive their hospitality.)

When you eat your fill, when you build and occupy good houses, when your cattle and flocks increase, when you have plenty of silver and gold, and when you have abundance of everything, be sure you do not feel self-important and forget the LORD your God who brought you from the land of Egypt, the place of slavery, and who brought you through the great, fearful wilderness of venomous serpents and scorpions, an arid place with no water. He made water flow from a flint rock and fed you in the wilderness with manna (which your ancestors had never before known) so that he might by humbling you test you and eventually bring good to you. Be careful not to say, "My own ability and skill have gotten me this wealth." You must remember the LORD your God, for he is the one who gives ability to get wealth; if you do this he will confirm his covenant that he

made by oath to your ancestors, even as he has to
this day.

Deuteronomy 8:12–18 NET

Human beings may not be at any greater risk for spiritual dryness than when life is going really well and we have very few needs. Seasons of ease can put us in a dangerous disposition spiritually. We're forgetful creatures. Abundance can leave us filled with plenty and empty of memories of God's goodness. Despite the acts of power and provision God has done in our lives, we have a propensity to forget. Even as we gather around full tables *at Thanksgiving*, it can be easy to take things for granted and to forget the One it all comes from.

What is something God has done in your life that you haven't thought about in a long time? Make a list of the ways He has provided or shown up.

The context of today's Scripture passage is that the nation of Israel had been rescued from hundreds of years of slavery in Egypt. Enough generations had been enslaved that all they knew was pain and oppression. Then God acted with a mighty hand and an outstretched arm and dramatically rescued them. He showed His power and glory to them by releasing their binds of slavery and leading them out to bind them to Himself in relationship. But God knows humankind, and He warned them not to forget all that He'd done. But they did forget. Over and over again. They complained and grumbled and questioned God's love for them and ability to provide.

To forget God's goodness and grace on our behalf is a sad type of spiritual memory loss that causes space between the creator God and created human beings.

What part of your life do you tend to grumble about often? Is there any connection between what you tend to complain about and something you've forgotten God has done for you?

If your life is filled with plenty—and most of our lives are—that's nothing to be ashamed of. What a gift from God to have enough food, clothing, shelter, work, and friendship! But can we heed the warning in this word from God through His servant Moses? The time when we're prone to forget God and His goodness is "when you have abundance of everything." When life is going fairly well, we can absentmindedly start feeling entitled to what we have instead of mindfully realizing it comes from Him.

Instead of allowing our abundance to bring absentmindedness, let's practice mindful thanksgiving, remembering God's good gifts.

God, You alone have given me everything I have. It's Your power and wisdom and faithfulness that have given me this family, this home, my most recent meal, the clothes on my body. While I have struggles and sorrows, You have brought me through so much in my life. Seasons of confusion and change, of hardship, of loneliness. In my current season, I thank You for Your gifts and look to You as the provider of every good thing. Thank You for Your provision, and bind me to You. Amen.

What are some simple symbols of what God has done in your life that you can set up around your home? Strategically place these photos or objects on mantels, bookshelves, kitchen windowsills, or in entryways to catch your eye and cause you to worship and remember God's faithfulness.

A GOOD YEAR

 Visit one of your social media pages. Take a moment to receive this powerful visual reminder of the photos, the videos, the insights you experienced and shared in the past year. Zero in on the things that were good and life-giving, even if there was a lot that was hard. Let the wonder of this year sink in.

> Devote yourselves to prayer, being watchful and thankful.
>
> Colossians 4:2

Life moves fast. Too fast, sometimes, and it's all we can do to keep up. We rush through Thanksgiving and then it's on to Christmas and the New Year, and before we know it three months have passed and all we've done is run at a rapid pace.

Sometimes—many times—the best thing we can do is to be fully present as we reflect on the year and what God has been saying to us. So let's do just that.

At this very moment, you are alive and you're free and healthy enough to open this book and take time for thought and reflection. Perhaps you're sipping your favorite drink while your cat is curled up at your feet. Perhaps you're in your favorite chair or you're on a plane or in a hospital or at the office.

You have shelter. Warmth. Food in the kitchen. A caring friend either gifted you this book or you had the resources to buy it. You're in control of your time to some degree, and you've chosen to sit down with us and think about the ways of God.

What are you thankful for right now?

This last year was difficult, no doubt about it. But there was good too. What was good? What memories will you take with you?

What happened this year that gives you hope and encouragement?

How did you learn and grow?

How did God guide and protect you this year?

We hope this exercise is beneficial as you step into this busy season that offers so much beauty. We hope it allows you to *see*—to truly see your life from the perspective of what God is doing and how He's moving.

Colossians 4:2 tells us to be prayerful, watchful, and thankful. In essence, to converse with God regularly, to see the world through

His eyes, and to offer up gratitude for who He is and how He's moving. This heart posture is so important because we can't acknowledge what we aren't seeing, and we can't see what we aren't looking for. When we slow down by praying, watching, thanking, He reveals so much more to us! And we're able to draw closer to Him.

Father, thank You for all that You have done and are doing this year. Thank You for Your provision and protection, for Your guidance and love. Open my eyes to see all that You're doing, that I may overflow with gratitude.

Reflect on your answers to today's questions. How is God moving and speaking? Take some time to write the story God has been telling through your life in the past year.

GRATITUDE EVEN NOW

Pay attention to the chaos of life—whatever that may mean for you, whatever is going on around you. Loud children, demanding employer, bursting email inbox, messy house, traffic noise, crowded public park. Allow yourself to be fully present, even if the experience is unpleasant or difficult. Then, transition to a place of quiet as you continue today's entry.

> Rejoice always, pray continually, give thanks in all circumstances; for this is God's will for you in Christ Jesus.
>
> 1 Thessalonians 5:16–18

"What are you thankful for?"

It's a common question asked around the Thanksgiving table. We may respond that we're thankful for our health or for our family. We may be thankful for something we are looking forward to or relieved that we were able to move past something hard.

Have you given thought to what you might share if asked the question this Thanksgiving?

There's so much that deserves all our gratitude, but there's something eye-opening about this typical approach to thankfulness. This question-and-response approach assumes two things: that our gratitude is tied to something in the past, and that gratitude is something that happens *to* us rather than something birthed *from* us.

Gratitude isn't merely a feeling. It's a way of living. It's a day-in, day-out lifestyle, something we should implement even in the midst of hardship and chaos, as James wrote: "Consider it pure joy, my brothers and sisters, whenever you face trials of many kinds" (James 1:2).

When there's so much going on around us, we can choose gratitude.

When we find ourselves overwhelmed by life and all that it brings, we can respond with a thankful posture.

And we can exercise this now, during this festive week that brings with it so much hope and, if we're honest, so much stress.

We can pause as we sit among relatives on Thanksgiving Day. We can slow our breath. We can remember the ever-presence of Christ. We can relax our jaw, shoulders, hands. We can create a moment of thanksgiving, feeling it well up within us and then pour out of us. We can see everything and everyone around us with eyes awakened to appreciation.

How might this posture change the way you live and engage with the things that are hard? Be specific.

Without changing anything on the outside, we can invite the change that gratitude brings on the inside. So, instead of reverting to that popular Thanksgiving table question, we may instead choose to ask, "How are you practicing gratitude today?" or "What in your life is drawing you into deeper gratitude?"

And you may be surprised by the answers you find.

> *God, in the midst of all that is around me, I pause to turn my attention to You. I know that none of the things in my life need to change for me to experience lightness and joy*

and thanksgiving right now. Your presence changes all of it. You allow my chaotic reality to become a quiet refuge. Open my heart and eyes to the gifts right in front of me. Amen.

Return to that place of chaos, where you tend to feel anything but grateful, and try the following practice. Pause, slow your breath, remember the presence of Christ, relax. Make room for thanksgiving and choose to see the situation and people around you with awakened appreciation.

A SUPPER OF THANKS

 Make yourself a piece of buttered toast or grab a few crackers. Spend a few moments quietly taking bites of your small snack. What do you taste? How would you describe it? What is the texture on your tongue? Try to mentally stay with the food in your mouth the whole time you're chewing and as you swallow, moving the food down into your stomach.

> For I received from the Lord what I also passed on to you: The Lord Jesus, on the night he was betrayed, took bread, and when he had given thanks, he broke it and said, "This is my body, which is for you; do this in remembrance of me." In the same way, after supper he took the cup, saying, "This cup is the new covenant in my blood; do this, whenever you drink it, in remembrance of me." For whenever you eat this bread and drink this cup, you proclaim the Lord's death until he comes.
>
> 1 Corinthians 11:23–26

Many churches include in their liturgy the sacrament of the Lord's Supper or Communion. Some do this every week while others have it as a special occasion. Jesus didn't tell us how often to practice it, but He did invite us to His table. He said "whenever" we eat the bread and drink the cup, we remember His body broken and His blood shed for us until He returns.

It's incredible to think that Jesus instituted this sacrament two thousand years ago, and it's still practiced by the church today. Some church communities call it the Eucharist. It comes from the Greek word that is translated into English in this passage as "given thanks." The Greek word is *eucharisteó*.

Do you regularly and intentionally give thanks? What would it look like in your life to do this every day and not just annually?

Building a habit of giving thanks is supported by research. Experts in the fields of psychology and neuroscience know that gratitude has the potential to alter our brain's chemistry. By making new, quicker connections to the feel-good center of the brain, gratitude increases neurotransmitters like dopamine and serotonin, regulates stress hormones, and encourages positive neural pathways.[4] And followers of Jesus know from Scripture that giving thanks is following in the footsteps of our King Jesus. Jesus's vibrant relationship with His Father was one of receiving *everything* from Him and responding with childlike faith and thanksgiving.

When Jesus multiplied the fish and the loaves to feed a crowd, He first took the humble meal and looked to His Father and gave thanks (Matthew 14:19). At the Last Supper with His disciples, in holding the bread and the cup and giving thanks, Jesus not only invited us to thank God regularly for the broken body and spilled blood that brought our redemption but also invited us into a countercultural practice He did as a human on earth. Remember, Jesus ate this meal with His disciples *before* His death on the cross. He made the connection between the elements and His body and blood. He invites us to look at what's painful and difficult in our lives, even death, and to look to Father God and say thank you—and anticipate resurrection life.

What is the hardest thing in your life to say thank you for right now?

The invitation to join Jesus in giving thanks is about communion with Him. But it isn't just for our personal benefit. It is meant to be corporate, an expression within our church communities that links all believers of different traditions and denominations. The Eucharist connects each of us with the historical and global church. Each time we eat the bread and drink the cup, we receive His body and become the body of Christ.

Because of the differences in time and culture, there's very little that believers from the time of Jesus would recognize today about a modern church gathering. If they were transported here, they'd have no idea what was going on during our foyer mingling with coffee cups in hand. They wouldn't know what the sermon was all about because of the language barrier. Our music might or might not look like worship to them. But the second the bread (or crackers in many cases) and grape juice came out, they'd know what was going on. Grateful faces with bread and wine in hand, gathered together to bow and give thanks and eat. Jesus followers from the distant past would know they were in the presence of the body of Christ: His body broken and His body gathered.

Jesus, as we celebrate Thanksgiving, I recognize that You invite me into a regular practice of thanksgiving at Your Table. You are Host to the family of God, made up of Your followers around the world and throughout church history. Would You allow me to feel more a part of Your kingdom and family than ever before? Would You allow that kinship to comfort me and give me courage? I join all of those brothers and sisters and say thank You. Thank You for Your broken body and Your shed blood that draw me into eternal fellowship. Amen.

Sense of Wonder

The next time you're at a gathering of the church that practices receiving Communion, consider all that's going on around you. It's a common part of the human experience to feel lonely, but how can you see yourself as part of a larger community, the church, as you receive the elements with thanksgiving? As you eat the bread and drink the cup, remember that you're a part of the historical and global body of Christ. How can you do your next activity today aware of your belonging in the kingdom? A part of something bigger?

OPEN INVITATION

 Put yourself in a posture of openness, whether it means lighting a candle, bowing at your bedside, or feeling fresh air on your face. What difficult emotions are you experiencing, if any? What feels hard right now? Where does God seem silent?

> Be still before the LORD
>   and wait patiently for him;
> do not fret when people succeed in their ways,
>   when they carry out their wicked schemes.
>
> Psalm 37:7

A family was in danger. For nearly a year and from thousands of miles away, I had been working to help get them to safety. God was moving. I was connected with a lawyer, there was financial support from others, and even the overflow of God's Spirit in other areas of my life all pointed to His presence and provision. Everything seemed as though God was preparing a great victory.

But then? The movement shifted. Our pleas to the government were denied. We had few options left—none that the family was interested in.

I remember thinking, *How can I express gratitude over this holiday season when so much is not right in the world? When my brothers and sisters are suffering and God seems silent?*

Even though I knew God to be faithful, I had a hard time receiving that from Him in those moments. All I could see were the things He hadn't done—the ways it seemed He'd failed or overlooked the needs of His people. And I was anything but thankful.

How have you felt that God has failed you recently? Try to open yourself up to vulnerability—even if what you're feeling may seem "unchristian."

This wrestling with God can stir up a lot within us, and one of the most common feelings is shame. Acknowledging a lack of trust in God can feel like we're faking our faith. But what would happen if we shifted our way of thinking? What if we assumed the best of God instead of the worst? What if we acknowledged that not only can He handle our frustration, but He's also moving and working for good, even now?

Perhaps we'd see the problem isn't that God is distant or silent. Perhaps the problem is in how we receive the King.

Many times, God is like a friend we invite to dinner only when He's on His best behavior. Only when He's talking and acting and looking the way we want Him to. But this isn't much of a relationship, is it? And it certainly isn't the type of friendship that will stand the test of time.

By practicing gratitude—a simple thankfulness for God's presence and trust in His promises—we can learn how to welcome the King even when we're struggling with Him. We can open our hands, open our hearts, and say, "God, I don't know why You're moving the way that You are, but I welcome You and I trust You and *today I choose You.*"

When the Israelites were fleeing from slavery in Egypt and came to the Red Sea—when they'd literally run into an insurmountable obstacle—God's instructions were clear: "The LORD will fight for you; you need only to be still" (Exodus 14:14).

Isn't this striking? They had come to a dead end, and God's desire was for them to be still. To wait on Him in the midst of their anxiety, fear, and worry. Psalm 37:7 builds on this, saying that we shouldn't give much thought to the success of the wicked. Rather, we are to wait and trust and *be still.*

As we change our approach to gratitude—as we move away from it being something we feel and instead turn it into something we practice—we'll change how we receive the King in our day-to-day. He'll be a friend we welcome with open arms rather than one we send an occasional invitation.

What can you do to have an open-door policy with the King of Kings?

Considering the hard things in your life, how might God be moving and working while you're standing still on the banks of the Red Sea? How might He be present in ways that aren't as noticeable when you're looking from a limited perspective?

Lord, here is my open invitation. Take it and keep it and know that You're always welcome in my heart and life. I welcome You even when it's hard for me to hear You. Even when I'm frustrated by what's around me. Even when things don't go the way I'd like. I welcome You, and I invite You, and I long to keep this openness even when I'm anxious or depressed or frustrated. Show me the ways that I tend to rescind my invitation to You. Work on my heart, O God, so that I trust and follow You even when I don't understand. Even when I'm waiting for You to move.

Write God an invitation, welcoming Him back to the table. Specifically list the hard things you're facing, and give those over to Him.

A LIFE LIVED FOR HIM

Notice the different textures around you. The rough brick wall, the knotted wood table, the knitted throw, the smooth pages of this book. Consider the beauty found in the world around you—beauty as simple as the difference in the way things feel.

> Through Jesus, therefore, let us continually offer to God a sacrifice of praise—the fruit of lips that openly profess his name.
>
> Hebrews 13:15

Life, with all its hardship, is beautiful. It's messy and disappointing and heartbreaking, yes—and also lovely. This can be a striking realization when you're walking through pain or difficulty. It can feel wrong to laugh when you're also grieving. To be overcome by the love found in community with other believers when at the very same time life feels so lonely. To be mesmerized by a sunset when you're also consumed by pain. To look forward to Thanksgiving gatherings when the family has also gone through loss.

How is your life hard but also beautiful?

Beauty that we sense in the midst of painful experiences is one way we receive gifts from our Savior—small reminders that He's present and He's active and there's so much more to His plan than we could ever fathom. They also remind us that He's with us and meets us right where we are.

There's so much beauty to be found in a walk through the woods or a porch conversation with a friend. And there's also beauty in a life lived for Him. *We* can create beauty wherever we go. In one of his sermons, Eugene Peterson wrote, "Beauty is our sensory access to holiness."[5] Think about that! Beauty—especially in hardship—can be a direct connection to that which is other and exceptional. Seeing beauty gives space for our pain and darkness to be reshaped by the reality of God's existence.

A life lived for Jesus—a life in tune with beauty and therefore holiness—is the ultimate movement of thankfulness to the Creator of all. It's the best response we can give Him to thank Him for a sunset, for friendship, for His sacrifice on the cross and His kingdom to come.

How can you put yourself in the path of beauty today?

How can your life become more of a living offering of praise and gratitude? Would your life be different if you spent a couple moments listening to worship music every day? If you chose to watch or listen to something beautiful to be reminded of God's beauty? How would it change every day to text a friend something you notice in life that is beautiful and to share that the reason is God's goodness?

Thank You for these moments, for time spent with You.
Thank You for the little reminders every day of Your
goodness. Reminders in the sunrise and sunset. In the

breeze. In time with friends. In gestures of compassion and love from others. Thank You for all of that. I pray that my life would be a continuation of Your beauty, Jesus. That through me, people would see and experience Your goodness and kindness, and that they are drawn closer to You.

As you go about your day today, look for God in the beauty around you—even if (especially if!) life is particularly hard right now. Thank God in three ways: thank Him for the beauty of His creation, thank Him for the love of His community (the church), and thank Him for your life as you use it to touch or help someone else.

ADVENT

Advent may or may not be familiar to you depending on your church experience and tradition, but it has been present in the life of the church for a very long time. Advent practices were mentioned as early as AD 380 at the Council of Saragossa in the church in the East, and the Western church has record of Advent-related sermons going back to the fifth century.

The word *Advent* comes from the Latin *adventus*, and it signifies a coming or arrival. It's a season of preparation and expectation, and it aims to bring our attention to three spaces of anticipation: Jesus's coming as an infant in Bethlehem, His coming again to make the world right, and His coming in our hearts and lives in this particular moment today. This powerful message should compel us to confess our sins, prepare our hearts, and turn our eyes to Jesus. Yet if the store shelves are any indication, this anticipation for His return has become lost. Today, Advent is a beer calendar or a piece of holiday decor. It's a few sermons in December and a few candles in a wreath. The truth and beauty behind this practice have been swallowed by our culture, and Advent has become something we buy or passively experience when it could be so much more.

This book offers an opportunity for Advent to be more.

The four Sundays of Advent have various traditions attached to them. For the sake of this book, we've drawn from the common practice of attributing to each of the Advent weeks a different theme: hope, peace, joy, and love. We've provided enough entries (seven for each theme) so you can engage one per day during the four weeks of Advent, starting on November 27. Or perhaps you may choose to read a single entry every Sunday, giving you enough content to make this book a part of your Advent practice for years to come.

May you fully engage with all that Advent means. May you reflect and remember that God sent His Son Jesus to earth two thousand years ago. May you prepare and expect His return and the restoration of the age to come. And may you experience His coming into your life today as you seek Him with all your senses.

WE HAVE HOPE

WHAT IS YOUR WILDEST HOPE?

Find a spice or flavor in the kitchen that you can quickly taste. A dab of cinnamon. A teaspoon of honey. An olive or even a bit of olive oil. Think about how this one ingredient is also a hint of a more elaborate recipe or dessert. It is almost a foretaste. Sure, cinnamon is good, but it's really good when mixed with pumpkin. Olive oil is rich on its own, but in a pasta dish it takes on new life. A small taste that points to a later, greater satisfaction of hunger.

> Jesus rebuked the demon, and it came out of the boy, and he was healed at that moment.
>
> Then the disciples came to Jesus in private and asked, "Why couldn't we drive it out?"
>
> He replied, "Because you have so little faith. Truly I tell you, if you have faith as small as a mustard seed, you can say to this mountain, 'Move from here to there,' and it will move. Nothing will be impossible for you."
>
> Matthew 17:18–20

Hope. It's the expectation of good things to come. A belief that all will be well. A desire for wholeness and completion, that the world and everything and everyone in it will be restored, even while there is hard evidence that it has not happened yet. *Yet.* Hope is the "yet."

What are some things, big or small, that you're hoping for right now?

Humans are born with a propensity toward hope. We hope for good to come out of the bad. We hope for happiness and wholeness. We hope for success and peace and sunny days ahead. But after a few times of having our hopes dashed to pieces, if we're honest, we often hold back in our hope. We play it safe, discarding our wildest hopes and replacing them with hope that feels more realistic. Practical. More likely to happen.

Think again of what you hope for. What are some wild, big hopes you didn't write down before? Especially think of hopes and dreams that you feel God has given you but you're hesitant to claim.

We play it safe with hope because we don't want to be disappointed in what does or doesn't happen. But God isn't a God of cautious hope!

God put every bit of hope for humanity's redemption into the form of a fragile, needy, helpless baby. Think about it! The source of salvation, completely reliant on others to ensure His safety, growth, protection. Doesn't that seem a bit reckless? It certainly seems wild! And doesn't that also show His power?

The best way we can be daring and bold in our hope is through prayer. When Jesus instructed His disciples to command the mountain to move in Matthew 17:20, He was instructing them to pray. To boldly ask God for the thing that would bring His power and kingdom into the world.

As we enter into this first week of Advent, let's remember this! The hope we have in Him is like nothing this world could ever offer. He did and does choose the most unlikely ways to exhibit His majesty. If God can handle putting the weight of the world on the shoulders of a tiny baby, then, my friend, He can handle your wildest, most honest hopes and dreams. He can handle your big prayers.

And that truth gives immeasurable hope.

> *Lord, You are the waymaker. The universe moves and responds to Your commands, and You are all-powerful, all-knowing, so much so that You can make the impossible possible. I claim this in my life today and every day. I ask for You to move and for me to rest in the hope that I have in Your power and goodness.*

Historically, the church has fasted during these weeks of Advent. Fasting is a way to refocus ourselves, turn to God in desperation, and experience hope in Him. Consider if there is a step you can take to incorporate fasting. Experiment with cultivating desperation for God by refraining from something that brings comfort. It can be anything you rely on or even something you tend to put your hope in. A treat. A meal. Coffee from the drive-through in the morning. Even scrolling on your phone. (Fasting from food is not for everyone in every season. Please seek wisdom from others if this is a potential area of struggle.)

NOT FEELING FESTIVE

 Burn some incense or spritz a calming fragrance. Breathe deeply, eyes closed. Explore where your mind, your heart, and especially your longings are. As Jesus often asked, "What do you want?" What are you longing for, aching for?

As the deer pants for streams of water,
    so my soul pants for you, my God.
My soul thirsts for God, for the living God.
    When can I go and meet with God?
My tears have been my food
    day and night,
while people say to me all day long,
    "Where is your God?"
These things I remember
    as I pour out my soul:
how I used to go to the house of God
    under the protection of the Mighty One
with shouts of joy and praise
    among the festive throng.

Why, my soul, are you downcast?
    Why so disturbed within me?
Put your hope in God,
    for I will yet praise him,
    my Savior and my God.

Psalm 42:1–5

That feeling. Sometimes it can be strong and consuming. Other times it's like an ache in your joints, revealing itself when you get up to move.

The feeling is longing. Disappointment, even. Sorrow.

The feeling may come and go. It may linger for a while or briefly visit before it moves on. But no matter how long it stays or how heavy it feels, we often wonder why this feeling comes at all.

Are you experiencing this now? Or perhaps you've experienced it in the past? Write about it here.

It seems silly almost, but it's possible to be surrounded by loved ones, by laughter, by good food and good times—and still feel as though something is missing. It's possible to be downcast when everyone and everything around you is so positive and joyful. At times we can pinpoint the reason we have this sense of longing or sadness, but sometimes there's no simple explanation for it. We long for more and don't know why.

What does it feel like when you long for more? Can you put it into words?

When we have feelings of longing, feasting can be extremely difficult. A merry Christmas feels far off. Making memories can seem irrelevant. It feels nearly impossible to put on the right face and enter into the festivities of the season.

Why is this? Why can there be so much missing in our internal world when so much good is going on in our external world? At those times, it can feel like there is something intrinsically wrong with us.

The psalmist in Psalm 42 reveals that these feelings of longing are due to the natural thirst we have for the living God. And instead of using that knowledge as a bandage to try to stop the bleeding and "move on," the psalmist does something interesting. The poet sits in that dichotomy of longing for more and yet knowing that *more* can be found in our Father in heaven.

This feeling of longing we experience is an invitation to come to the Lord in prayer. The hunger or sense of need we feel should be presented before God. Not just when the idea strikes or when the feelings become too much. We should present our longings to Him from the moment they begin to bubble up to well after they've subsided.

This is what the psalmist practiced—a constant conversation with God, no matter the feelings that overwhelmed. And at the end of his psalm, he boldly declared that his hope was in God even though he still felt downcast and lost.

Instead of pushing our feelings aside as the holidays swell, let's take them to the One who always has capacity to hold our emotions. Instead of expecting the holiday season to satisfy our longing, let's go to Him who alone can satisfy. And if the festive season doesn't bring positive feelings, let's use that to drive us to our God, the source of real hope.

As long as we're on this earth, in these bodies, we will have longings. We will have longings because we aren't whole.

So let's go to the only One who can fill us.

I join the psalmist in crying out to You, God. You are worthy of worship, and Your gifts are worth celebrating. I know feasting with joy is appropriate, but I need something more than the food before me. I need what only You can provide. God of hope, fill me with all joy and peace as I trust in You, that I may overflow with hope by the power of Your Holy Spirit. Amen.

When feelings of longing or unexplained sorrow creep in, set your to-do list aside and instead spend that time in prayer.

Sense of Wonder

HOPE EVEN IN FAILURE

Wrap yourself in a blanket. Feel the security and warmth it brings. Feel the weight the blanket creates and let it ground you. Imagine being held by the arms of God.

> The LORD had said to Abram, "Go from your country, your people and your father's household to the land I will show you.
>
> "I will make you into a great nation,
>   and I will bless you;
> I will make your name great,
>   and you will be a blessing.
> I will bless those who bless you,
>   and whoever curses you I will curse;
> and all peoples on earth
>   will be blessed through you."
>
> Genesis 12:1–3

Abraham. Isaac. Jacob. Joseph. When you read these names, what comes to mind?

These men are revered in the Christian and Jewish faiths. Rightfully so! God showed them favor. They allowed God to move through them and work in them. They saw miracles because of their faithfulness, and the Christian faith exists as it does today because they entered into what God was doing and chose to walk with Him. They were blessed and, in turn, became a blessing to the world.

But these men were also part of an extremely dysfunctional family. Abraham became impatient for God's promise for a son, so he and his wife, Sarah, hatched a plan for him to sleep with her slave (Genesis 16). Jacob tricked his father, Isaac, into giving him the family blessing (Genesis 27), and Joseph's brothers tried to murder him (Genesis 37). And these were just a few of the schemes that got them in trouble!

When you're looking for them, the flaws of this family stand out. Their missteps, disobedience, and lack of faith seem to be all over the pages of the Old Testament. You may even come away wondering why God chose—and continued to choose—such a problematic family. How could God's favor rest on that type of dysfunction?

There's a lesson here that is both powerful and freeing.

God chose the family of Abraham over and over. Not because of their perfect lives but because of the covenant—the promise—He had made with them. Though Abraham and later the nation of Israel were unable to hold up their end of the covenant, God could! Hope wasn't in their obedience and faithfulness but in God's loyal love and commitment to His promise. Through this, we see that if there was hope and purpose for this imperfect family, then there's hope and purpose for us. God maintains His blessing even when we're faithless.

Take a moment and think of something you've done that feels shameful. Write it here or hint at it here.

The hope Jesus offers us is this: *the shameful thing you did does not disqualify you from a life of blessing.*

God has a plan for you. God is inviting you into a life of meaning and jaw-dropping surprises. Yes, we make mistakes. Yes, we fall short.

But the hope offered to us says that God is faithful. And if He can take broken, damaged people like Abraham, Isaac, Jacob, and Joseph and turn them into patriarchs of the faith, then He can do incredible things in our lives and bless others through us! And that is a hope worth living for.

Lord, You are the hope that the world needs! You look past all our shame, all our bad, all our shortcomings, and You see Your sons and daughters whom You love and have big plans for. Help me to see those plans and not my shame. Help me to remember Your faithfulness and not my faithlessness. Help me to see that Your story of hope outweighs my moments of losing heart. Help me to move forward, fully claiming the hope I have for a life lived for You.

Today, what is a small act, something that's been on your mind, that you feel God has planned for you? Write it down, and then do it! Call that friend, volunteer with that organization, lead that group. Step forward, knowing that your failures or shortcomings don't define God's plan for your life.

DO WE LIVE WITH HOPE FOR TODAY?

 Find a quiet place of solitude and listen to "Night Has Passed" by The Brilliance. (There's a lyric video for the song on YouTube, which is free.)

> And we know that in all things God works for the good of those who love him, who have been called according to his purpose.
>
> Romans 8:28

Romans 8:28 is a verse of hope and reassurance, comfort and proclamation. It's almost like a sigh of relief. God is at work in our lives, and all we need to do is love Him.

If this verse is familiar to you, what are your first memories of it? If it's unfamiliar, what thoughts and feelings does the verse bring about within you?

At face value, the verse makes life sound so easy, doesn't it? God is at work, so we should live boldly, without fear or worry. We should always trust that things will work out and always give them over to

God. After all, doesn't the end of Psalm 84:11 state, "No good thing does he withhold from those whose walk is blameless"?

But is that realistic? Is that what God really expects of us? Let's zoom out and look at the paragraph leading up to verse 28.

> In the same way, the Spirit helps us in our weakness. We do not know what we ought to pray for, but the Spirit himself intercedes for us through wordless groans. And he who searches our hearts knows the mind of the Spirit, because the Spirit intercedes for God's people in accordance with the will of God.
>
> And we know that in all things God works for the good of those who love him, who have been called according to his purpose. (vv. 26–28)

God doesn't expect us to go through life with steeled resolve, not letting anything bother us. Rather, this passage makes it clear that things *should* bother us! We're to feel deeply about life and all that is broken around us. We're to feel an urgency for God's kingdom to come and for all things to be made right.

And in this state of need for God, that is when we receive the comforting of the Spirit—our very best friend, who is with us in our pain and worry and sadness. (In John 16:7, in the King James Version, Jesus even referred to His Spirit as the Comforter!)

We can know that God is at work and that He will make all things right, and we can still feel burdened, overwhelmed, and even hopeless at times. All of these emotions are possible for people who love and follow Jesus.

How freeing this is!

The Holy Spirit is calling us to Him. He wants to be in it with us, whatever we're going through. He wants us to feel deeply about kingdom things and to approach God's throne even when we don't have the words.

While many use Romans 8:28 as an excuse to "let go and let God," let's instead use it as the reason to involve ourselves in the messiness of life. To feel deeply about it and to live with the beautiful hope that God is at work and that our groans and actions don't go unnoticed.

How can you better live out Romans 8:26–28 this holiday season? What situation or person or thing have you been avoiding?

Father, You love it when I feel deeply about the things that matter—when I'm burdened by the things that burden You. Help me to lean into this. Help me to rest in the Holy Spirit, to embrace the hope and comfort found in Him, and to recognize that a life of faith doesn't mean a life of flippancy. A life of faith is deeply rooted in desiring and chasing after the things that are most important to You. Help me to embrace that and find refreshed hope as I seek Your kingdom.

When you come across something in your day that feels difficult and troublesome—something that feels not right—stop. Remind yourself that while God is active and at work, He also invites us to fully participate and partner with Him. So instead of simply giving it over to Him or freezing in your tracks, *choose action.* Step into the brokenness of the situation with hope that by His Spirit, you can bring healing and life where there's pain.

DO WE LONG FOR JESUS'S RETURN?

What is a snack or beverage that you look forward to? A piece of chocolate in the evening? A cup of tea in the afternoon? A slice of pie you set aside for later? Prepare a bit of that now or make a plan to have that later in your day. As you taste it, think about what it's like to wait for that bit of pleasure in your day.

> He has appeared once for all at the end of the ages to put away sin by the sacrifice of himself. And just as it is appointed for man to die once, and after that comes judgment, so Christ, having been offered once to bear the sins of many, will appear a second time, not to deal with sin but to save those who are eagerly waiting for him.
>
> Hebrews 9:26–28 ESV

The disciples eagerly anticipated Jesus's return. They expected it, as if it could happen that very day, that very hour. *And they welcomed it.* They prepared for it. They felt an urgency around it and believed it would happen in their lifetime.

When you think about the return of Christ, what emotions and feelings well up within you? Are you eager? Hesitant? Afraid? Apathetic? Confused?

It can be difficult to capture the same urgency the disciples had. Sure, it's been two thousand years since Jesus walked the earth, and momentum can be hard to maintain long term. But perhaps our lack of energy and expectancy has nothing to do with the amount of time that's passed or the fact that we never met Jesus in person.

Perhaps it's because we're thinking about His return in the wrong way.

It's easy to zero in on death and destruction, on fear and judgment. Those words rattle us! They cause us to feel big emotions.

But the message of God isn't about those things. The Bible story is a story for the meek. It's a story for the broken. It's a story for people in need of a gentle nudge more than a slap across the face.

It's a story of so much goodness toward humanity.

What if we shifted our perspective? What if we looked at Jesus's return not as a way for God to punish people but rather as a way for Him to restore the world?

What if we viewed it not as the end but as the beginning?

The Bible story is of a God-King who built a relationship with humanity and then came to earth so He could live and die and offer salvation through His resurrection and return. The story, when told by many preachers and speakers, ends there . . . but we are promised a sequel. The Bible even foreshadows it.

We're promised that His return will make everything right.

We're promised that His return will bring oneness with Him.

And we're promised life in the age to come, a life of purpose and meaningful work and relationships—all without brokenness!

Think about that. In the coming age, you will *live* as you've never lived before.

In this sense, the end times isn't the end. It's the beginning of something beautiful.

What if we lived with this hope today? How would our actions, thoughts, and choices be different if we lived with the knowledge that our story is just getting started? That the finish line isn't a singular point in time yet to come but a life lived for eternity and through eternity under the rule of the very King who came here to save us two thousand years ago?

How would this shift change the way you live life and hope in God?

Lord, my human understanding of Your goodness and Your plan can only take me so far. It can only do so much. And just when I think I have You figured out, I find how little I actually know—and how much I must trust. I see that the hope You offer is a place within the kingdom of God, where everything is made right and each and every one of us will thrive under Your love and care. Help me to live with that in mind. Help me to remember that the hope You offer isn't merely a way out of something bad but a way into something completely beautiful.

Spend some time thinking about the kingdom of God after the Lord's return. If you have time, read about the new heaven and new earth and what different Christian theologians believe life could be like beyond the "end times."

AN ABUNDANT LIFE

Find a quiet place and listen to "Promises" by Maverick City Music. Read or sing the lyrics.

The LORD is good to all;
   he has compassion on all he has made.
All your works praise you, LORD;
   your faithful people extol you.
They tell of the glory of your kingdom
   and speak of your might,
so that all people may know of your mighty acts
   and the glorious splendor of your kingdom.
Your kingdom is an everlasting kingdom,
   and your dominion endures through all generations.

The LORD is trustworthy in all he promises
   and faithful in all he does.

Psalm 145:9–13

Have you stopped lately to consider the promises of God? Here are just a few of the thousands of promises He's made to us:

He gives wisdom if we ask (James 1:5).
He gives direction (Proverbs 3:5–6).
He forgives us when we confess our sins (1 John 1:9).
He will never give up on us (Deuteronomy 31:6).
He will provide for us (Philippians 4:19).

He will answer when we call (Psalm 50:15).

He gives us freedom (John 8:36).

Which of God's promises (whether listed above or not) stand out to you?

It's convicting how much we value a promise from a friend—and how much we dismiss a promise from God. Our friends are broken, fallen, human. Yet we're more likely to rely on and trust a promise from them than we are to receive and trust that the living God will be true to His word.

God actually follows through. He does what He says He will do. He doesn't merely want to offer us salvation and a life made new after we die; He offers us a way to live *this* life to the fullest. He wants us to take advantage of each and every one of His promises!

Why is it so hard to remember this? Why do His promises feel so distant when we're in need of a breakthrough? And what would happen if we changed our approach?

A life on this earth with Jesus is a life of partnership, guidance, and community. We aren't left here to struggle through the brokenness and suffering of this world alone. God comes beside us—He's sent the Holy Spirit to work *within* us—and He is always good on His promises.

Let that truth fill you with renewed hope this holiday season. God wants you to live abundantly. Not in the sense of earthly recognition or wealth. But abundant in discernment. Abundant in joy. Abundant in love. Abundant in wisdom. Abundant in faith. Abundant in hope. Full of the riches of His promises and filled with His presence!

How can you claim God's promises and live in this abundance today? How might that change your life going forward?

God, thank You for Your promises—every one of them. You want to do life with me, and You've made a way for that to happen. I confess I don't always take You up on the offer. I confess there are times I doubt You'll follow through. Help me with my doubt. Help me to trust You. You have abundant life for me, even when I don't understand Your ways or see You move. You are faithful and You will come through.

Take one of God's promises and pull it into your day or week by writing it down. Claim it at the beginning of your day and put it somewhere that will bring it to mind throughout the rest of the day. Write down anything you notice as a result of this practice.

A BELIEVER'S PURPOSE

 Legs crossed, eyes closed, turn your palms up. Invite the Spirit to move in you, to fall fresh on you.

Then his wife told him, "Do you remain firm in your integrity? Curse God and die!"

But he replied to her, "You're talking like foolish women do. Are we to accept what is good from God but not tragedy?"

Throughout all of this, Job did not sin by what he said.

Job 2:9–11 ISV

Purpose. Our culture obsesses over it, and many are willing to pay lots of money to try to find it. When one does find it, typically it looks something like this:

My purpose in life is to grow a business.
My purpose is to raise a family.
My purpose is to create beauty.
My purpose is to inspire others.
My purpose is to create opportunity for others.
My purpose is to help those in need.

All of these things are wonderful and beautiful. And all of them are dangerously incomplete. What happens when the business fails? What happens when our family breaks apart? What happens when our health prevents us from making music or writing or painting? What happens when we're depressed? What happens when things don't go as planned?

What are some things you believe God has for you in this life? What is your purpose, if you will?

Considering the above, how would you respond if these things failed or didn't end up looking the way you thought they would?

It's easy to express gratitude and glorify God when life is going well. But what about when life falls apart? How can we be thankful and live with hopeful purpose when dreams are dashed to pieces, expectations are unmet, and our life turns out different than we planned?

The book of Job provides insight on this. Job's life is a reminder that our true purpose isn't to use our gifts or amass a legacy. Our true purpose is to glorify God, *no matter what*.

Job had it all, and in a blink of an eye it was gone. His family, his possessions, his notoriety, his health. Gone. Job was absolutely devastated, but he wouldn't curse God. He knew the most important thing was to glorify his Creator, even when life didn't go as planned.

Glorifying God looks like a life turned toward Him. It looks like open hands that say, "Open my eyes to whatever You have for me today, Lord." It looks like loosely held plans that leave room for God to rewrite the script. It looks like a faith and trust and hope that isn't built on the things of this world but on our love for God and others. It looks like kindness, compassion, gentleness, patience.

We may be gifted in music and art and creativity.

We may be successful in business and innovation.

We may have a way with children and caring for others.

And God may have big things in store for us because of these gifts and talents!

But our purpose—our true purpose—is to point back to Him with how we live. So even when we aren't creating or innovating or operating from an area of strength, God's presence is still abundantly felt in our lives.

We thank and praise Him because at the end of the day, He is what matters. He's *all* that matters, as Job made clear—and Advent is such a beautiful reminder of this. He's the hope of the world, and if we believe that, then we should live it out.

> *Father, I praise You for the gifts and talents and desires You've given me—and I offer them back to You. They are Yours. Use them in a big way or use them in a small way. And work on my heart. Help me to give these things to You daily. Help me to trust You with them, and help me to keep my focus on what matters—not what I'm doing for You but rather my heart posture along the way. I trust You and I praise and thank You for Your goodness. Your kindness. Your faithfulness.*

Consider the things you indicated above that you believe God is calling you to. Choose one of them and pursue it today in a way that may seem small, trusting that God sees your heart. As you prepare and offer that thing to Him, maintain a heart posture of gratitude and glory to God.

✦ Week Two of Advent ✦

WE HAVE PEACE

THE GREATNESS OF HIS GOVERNMENT

Turn on the news in some way. Stream it from your phone for a few moments or switch on a TV or radio.

For to us a child is born,
to us a son is given,
and the government will be on his shoulders.
And he will be called
Wonderful Counselor, Mighty God,
Everlasting Father, Prince of Peace.
Of the greatness of his government and peace
there will be no end.
He will reign on David's throne
and over his kingdom,
establishing and upholding it
with justice and righteousness
from that time on and forever.
The zeal of the Lord Almighty
will accomplish this.

Isaiah 9:6–7

Even in just a few minutes of listening to the news, it doesn't take long to get a barrage of troublesome headlines. Hurricanes. Wars and rumors of wars. Kidnappings. Conflict between tribes or political parties or countries. School shootings. Hollywood scandal. Church scandal. Corrupt businesses and inefficient governments. The world is broken and filled with trouble and pain. The holidays sometimes act as a glowing distraction from this reality, but there are too many reminders. No matter how many Christmassy Hallmark movies we watch, there's a deep realization that happy endings aren't guaranteed in human experience.

Brokenness is nothing new. When Isaiah prophesied the words of Isaiah 9:6–7, the world was broken. Seven hundred years later, when Jesus came as a fragile infant, the world was broken. Today, two thousand years after that, much has changed, yet the world is still incredibly broken.

Jesus established a government that is the general solution for global brokenness, then and now. His government is for these particular headlines and these heartaches. To us, in this day and age, a child has been born. And our only chance for peace, in this world and in our hearts, is this child. During the holidays, and at all other times of the year for that matter, the only potential for real peace is found in a Wonderful Counselor, a Mighty God, and an Everlasting Father. The Prince of Peace.

What is a headline that is on your mind and heart these days? Where is a place in the world today that needs the rule of the Prince of Peace?

Pay attention to your internal world, your emotions. Where is a place in your heart today that needs the rule of the Prince of Peace?

It's tempting to want to cover our ears and put on blinders to avoid the pain all over the world. But it can't be avoided, not even at a time of year marked for joy and peace. The only way to stay engaged in the hurting world around us and to not lose hope is to stay grounded in the reality of the greatness of Jesus's government. It isn't merely a coming kingdom someday, a castle in the clouds, but it's a reign He started after His birth and invites us into now!

We're invited to live under His kingship in our words and actions. We're promised His presence at all times in all parts of our lives. Every choice we make today is a part of establishing the reign of the Wonderful Counselor, Mighty God, Everlasting Father, Prince of Peace. This doesn't mean we'll escape temporary injustices, but we have a very real promise. His kingdom will be fully established, and it will never end. The government of the Prince of Peace is as real as today but as lasting as forever.

As I pray to You, God, I remember that You are the Wonderful Counselor, Mighty God, Everlasting Father, Prince of Peace. [Pause and take a few breaths.] The rulers of the earth are broken and limited in what they can accomplish, but You are what this world needs for peace and justice. Would Your kingdom come and Your will be done on earth as it is in heaven? I long for You to make all things right—in the world and in me. Show me a step to take today to live within Your kingdom ways of peace. Amen.

Remind someone who needs the peace of Christ today that Jesus is not only the baby in the manger and the Savior on the cross but also the Wonderful Counselor, Mighty God, Everlasting Father, Prince of Peace.

WAITING FOR HIS PRESENCE

 If possible, go outside for a few moments. Zip up a coat or grab an umbrella if you need. While standing, try to hold your body completely still, almost like you're in the suspense of waiting. Take a long inhale through your nose, smelling the air. Take a few more deep breaths in and out of your nose. Concentrate on the smell of the air. What words would you use to describe the aromas in the air?

> The LORD said, "Go out and stand on the mountain in the presence of the LORD, for the LORD is about to pass by."
>
> Then a great and powerful wind tore the mountains apart and shattered the rocks before the LORD, but the LORD was not in the wind. After the wind there was an earthquake, but the LORD was not in the earthquake. After the earthquake came a fire, but the LORD was not in the fire. And after the fire came a gentle whisper. When Elijah heard it, he pulled his cloak over his face and went out and stood at the mouth of the cave.
>
> Then a voice said to him, "What are you doing here, Elijah?"
>
> 1 Kings 19:11–13

In large part, Advent is a season of waiting. Come to think of it, most of the church calendar is crafted around the idea of waiting and anticipation. The year with its monotony and worry-filled schedule is regularly interrupted with set weeks of waiting. Wonder-filled waiting. For instance, this season of Advent builds up to and gives way to Jesus's incarnation, His birth. Lent is a season practiced in many church circles that leads up to His death on Good Friday and His resurrection on Easter Sunday. Throughout the year these spaces for waiting culminate in meaningful remembering or wild celebration. The church calendar is becoming increasingly precious to more and more denominations in part for this reason: waiting is a part of human experience.

Scripture is filled with characters who were in long seasons of waiting. Many of the psalms are about waiting and describe it so vividly, realistically, and even beautifully. And while waiting is difficult, it is the space between the chaos of circumstances and the peace of the presence of Jesus.

Let's look at Elijah's story from 1 Kings 19. Can you imagine actually being told by God to just stand and wait for Him? What would you expect? How would you feel? At this point in Elijah's life, he was in a place of desperation and despair in his calling as a prophet. Many opposed him, and a few wanted to kill him. He was at the end of his human ability and the proverbial rope, feeling both mentally and emotionally unstable. He was ready to quit not only his role and calling but also his life. He felt totally alone and abandoned by God.

Have you felt like this before? When was the last time?

This waiting for God was an unlikely mountaintop experience. "Mountaintop experience" usually connotes feelings of exhilaration and inspiration, where God reveals Himself in a way that matches our feelings of adrenaline and excitement. But that isn't the place or the state where God invited Elijah to meet with Him.

It was in desperation and depression that God requested to meet with him.

God draws near to the desperate and depressed—but He doesn't often swipe away difficult emotions and instantly replace them with peace. Of all the ways God could've revealed Himself to Elijah, He chose not to come right away. He chose to show Elijah where He is *not* before revealing Himself in a gentle whisper. Or as some translations say, "a still small voice." But this involved waiting. Waiting for the peace of God's presence.

When was a time this week that you were moving at a fast pace—either physically or mentally?

Is there a circumstance in your life where you are waiting for the Lord to encounter you with peace? Are you standing on any mountaintops, so to speak, waiting for God to meet you?

At this time of Advent, we're all waiting for His appearing, all waiting for the coming of Christmas. And even though waiting is not how we prefer to find Jesus, many times it's the method He chooses, because it's in our waiting that we're most laid bare. It allows Him to meet us exactly in that vulnerable state of in-between, where we more readily receive His peace.

> *God, I come to You now with my senses fully available*
> *to You. I can feel so alone and in need of You, as if I'm*

standing out on a mountain waiting for You to reveal
Your presence to me. There are times I look so hard for
You, but You are found at unlikely times and in unlikely
places. You invite me to pay attention all throughout the
day for the peaceful appearing of Your presence, the quiet
whisper of Your word. Forgive my hurry and resistance
to waiting that inhibit my connection with You. I pause
and remember that You are near, as close as my breath.

Take three to five minutes, now or later in your day, to just sit
and be still. Either alone or in plain view of others. Fight the urge
to seek God only in the spectacular and exciting. Be willing to
receive Him in the quiet and ordinary. Feel free to try this with
another person in order to invite them into this space of quiet.

WHAT KEEPS THE PEACE

 Visually meditate on the shape of a cross—either an object in your home or an artist's rendering of the crucifixion, or even draw a simple cross on paper to gaze at for a few minutes.

> Surely he took up our pain
>   and bore our suffering,
> yet we considered him punished by God,
>   stricken by him, and afflicted.
> But he was pierced for our transgressions,
>   he was crushed for our iniquities;
> the punishment that brought us peace was on him,
>   and by his wounds we are healed.
> We all, like sheep, have gone astray,
>   each of us has turned to our own way;
> and the Lord has laid on him
>   the iniquity of us all.
>
> Isaiah 53:4–6

It can be easy to take for granted the things we've been given that we didn't work for or earn. Many of us have worked hard for many things, but at the same time we have at least some possessions, safety, privileges, or abilities that we're not fully responsible for. They were given to us. Bestowed on us.

What are you currently working for or toward? How would you describe your work ethic?

As the holiday season builds momentum, do you find yourself working to keep the peace externally or internally? Are there situations and relationships you seem to have to hold together? Are there internal emotional states you work so hard to manage? There can be good, meaningful work that becomes an unhealthy striving. Jesus invites us into a posture of ceasing our striving. A posture of *receiving* the hard-won work He already accomplished.

There was an unbearably difficult work needed to remove the sin and brokenness that disrupted the peace God desires for human beings. Jesus did that work. The work was finished. A tired, broken, and bruised Jesus declared this in John 19:30 while on the cross: "It is finished."

Be as honest as you can. What determines you feeling at peace from day to day?

It's likely that some of our conditions and feelings about maintaining peace are transitory and fragile. If the peace around us is based on a work we do or the managing of our emotions, how can it last? Let's remember: Jesus joyfully worked to bring deep and lasting peace to our hearts and lives. Hebrews 12:2 says, "For the joy set before him he endured the cross, scorning its shame."

In our hard work of achieving in life, have we forgotten all that was achieved by the blood of Jesus? It was an outpouring of blood, sweat, and tears so powerful that it made way for an impossible peace.

Jesus's sacrificial act accomplished so much. So much has been written about His death on the cross, but let's focus on this one piece: the punishment that brought us peace. Nothing we could ever do maintains or diminishes that depth of peace. We can't keep the peace. Only Jesus's sacrifice can do that. Take a deep breath today, in the chaos around you, and remember this: the very essence of who you are, forever, is preserved safe and secure and at rest by the blood of Jesus. We have peace like a river deep in our soul.

Father, Son, and Holy Spirit, I pause now to cease striving for a moment. You know all that I'm working for in my life. You know my intentions and motives. Sometimes I can fool myself into thinking that I keep the peace inside my heart and mind and in the lives of those around me. Your work on the cross was powerful, and it is finished. The peace You accomplished isn't weak and flimsy but hard-won and bought by Your blood. I receive it. How can I offer that peace to others in Your name, Jesus?

Do you take a weekly rest? Sabbath is a concept as foreign to the American mindset as any, but it's very biblical and a part of life in His kingdom. Jesus practiced Sabbath. It's a way to receive the work Jesus did on the cross and the work God is doing all the time as the King of the universe. If you aren't in the habit of taking a day of rest each week, take an hour or two this week to turn off your phone, put aside your tasks and chores, and just do something relaxing or playful. Do this as an act of receiving the peace that Jesus provided through His work on the cross.

ELUSIVE OR PERVASIVE?

For a few moments, experience the dark. Ideally, find a closet or windowless room where you can turn off the lights and open your eyes in the dark. If this isn't possible, just close and cover your eyes and feel the dark.

> Where can I go from your Spirit?
>   Where can I flee from your presence?
> If I go up to the heavens, you are there;
>   if I make my bed in the depths, you are there.
> If I rise on the wings of the dawn,
>   if I settle on the far side of the sea,
> even there your hand will guide me,
>   your right hand will hold me fast.
> If I say, "Surely the darkness will hide me
>   and the light become night around me,"
> even the darkness will not be dark to you;
>   the night will shine like the day,
>   for darkness is as light to you.
>
> Psalm 139:7–12

Sometimes it seems like we live in a world where peace is hard to come by. This time of year, "peace" is on greeting cards and ornaments and even the occasional Christmas sweater, but that doesn't make it any more tangible in our actual lives. We long for it, but it can feel elusive. Sometimes even our own thoughts and emotions are in the way, making peace seem unreachable, unattainable.

The psalmists often talk about how great God is, how massive and powerful and mighty. But we also have access to ancient songs in the Psalms that are about God's nearness and intimacy. In this reading, we are reminded that God's nearness to us is available at every turn. Peace is available around every dark corner of the earth because God is available around every dark corner of the earth.

What is a space or a situation in your life right now where it's hard to imagine or sense God's nearness?

When in your past did you not feel God's presence, but in looking back you can see that He was near and providing in some way?

Throughout history, there are stories of believers who were in incredibly difficult and dark situations and could testify of the peace of God that truly surpassed all human logic and understanding. In concentration camps, in prisons, on plantations, in hiding, in hospital rooms. God has been seen and heard and His peace experienced in the darkest places by human beings who lived to tell about it. Peace doesn't get any more tangible than that.

Psalm 139:12 says that darkness and light are the same to God. What is a current situation that feels dark to you, a situation where you're unable to see clearly and maybe it's even scary?

Even there, in that place, the peace of God is available to you. God wants you to call on Him and look for Him everywhere you go.

Where can I go from Your Spirit? Where can I flee from Your presence? I call to mind, Lord, the places and moments that have felt far from You and remember that You were just as close to me then. I forget or overlook Your presence, but You never leave me. Your peace isn't elusive but pervasive. When I can't see in the dark, you see all, because Your presence is so full of holiness and brightness. Today I repeat these simple words as my prayer:"Even the darkness will not be dark to you; the night will shine like the day."

Who is someone in your life who's running from God or others? Pray for that person to find God in the midst of the darkness and to find His peace to be pervasive in his or her life. To help you remember to pray for the person, or just as a reminder for yourself, where could you put that simple prayer from Psalm 139:12? By a light switch or a lamp or a candle?

HE PREACHED PEACE

 If your diet, digestion, or pantry allows, eat something sweet as you begin today's devotion. Maybe a spoonful of honey or a piece of dark chocolate, or if you're really lucky and have a muffin or doughnut or cookie lying around, savor a few bites of sweetness. Before diving in and engaging your brain with words, allow your brain to process the taste and feel of that treat on your tongue.

> But now in Christ Jesus you who once were far away have been brought near by the blood of Christ.
>
> For he himself is our peace, who has made the two groups one and has destroyed the barrier, the dividing wall of hostility, by setting aside in his flesh the law with its commands and regulations. His purpose was to create in himself one new humanity out of the two, thus making peace, and in one body to reconcile both of them to God through the cross, by which he put to death their hostility. He came and preached peace to you who were far away and peace to those who were near. For through him we both have access to the Father by one Spirit.
>
> Ephesians 2:13–18

This time of year, we often remember Jesus as an infant, so let's take a moment in this season to consider His ministry as an adult. Have you ever thought of the effects Jesus's ministry and message had on people? Conversations around the topics of religion or doctrine or politics or theology can be incendiary to say the least. In reading any of the Gospels, the accounts of Jesus's life, it's clear that Jesus experienced a lot of opposition. Religious leaders in particular questioned and argued with and challenged Jesus a lot. Some were shocked and offended by what He preached and how He responded. However, His preaching was a proclamation of peace.

What are some preaching or teaching or TED-talking voices that you've heard? Are they voices of peace?

Some of the things Jesus said were challenging or convicting, a seemingly far cry from "good news of great joy for all the people" (Luke 2:10 ISV). But His good news of the kingdom was really good news for *all*. It meant that whether you were a Jew (like Jesus was and is) or a Gentile, you were invited to follow Him, receive new life in Him, and belong in His kingdom. This message was for those who were close (Jews) and those who were far (Gentiles). Even today, the message and voice of Jesus carries peace with it, and all who hear and receive it are given access by His Spirit to the Father.

Ephesians 2:13–18 mentions two groups (Jews and Gentiles) being made into one. What are two groups that come to mind that the good news of Jesus would allow to become one, having removed the barrier between them? That may sound unrealistic, but the Scriptures say Jesus is our peace and destroyed the dividing wall of hostility. What groups can you imagine finding peace together before the triune God?

Jesus, You are our peace. At the end of an argument at work, a conflict with someone close to me, an intense debate, or a rough day with children, I need to take a deep breath and remember that You are our peace. That despite strong opinions and stark differences, Your work on the cross removed the barrier between people, and it's Your work today that's still tearing down walls. I'm reminded of Your work of reconciliation and Your invitation to me to participate in it. Amen.

We all know the feeling of exclusion. The reality is that so many people experience a lack of belonging. Jesus preached peace and meant for all to be welcome to come to Him—and we're given that same ministry of reconciliation. This holiday season, who is someone in your midst who He would have you invite to the table, so to speak? Who would Jesus have you step closer toward, remembering that "he himself is our peace, who has made the two groups one"?

A HOLISTIC BLESSING

Wherever you're seated, starting at your toes, pay attention to each part of your body. Your feet, ankles, lower legs, knee joints. You get the idea. Go slowly and mindfully. Almost like taking a tour of your body. How is your body feeling? What needs does it have? What is your energy level like?

> May God himself, the God of peace, sanctify you through and through. May your whole spirit, soul and body be kept blameless at the coming of our Lord Jesus Christ. The one who calls you is faithful, and he will do it.
>
> 1 Thessalonians 5:23–24

This blessing given by Paul to the church in Thessalonica is so beautiful and comprehensive, so rich and pure. It calls forth blessing from the God of peace. How would you define *peace*?

An important idea in the mind of a Jew at the time of Jesus is that of the Hebrew word *shalom*. It means, in essence, "holistic flourishing." *Holistic* as in "in every way, at every level, through every layer." *Flourishing* as in "filled with truth, goodness, and beauty." Simply put: the way things should be. Even though the New Testament was written in Greek (not Hebrew), when the word "peace" is used by its

Jewish authors, it's pointing to this idea of God's. God's original plan for the whole world was for it to flourish in every way with Him as a very present King with His creation. Even now with the presence of sin and brokenness and death, this is still His mission. He's the God of peace who came in the flesh as a human person of peace to live the way of peace on the earth.

As a human representation of peace, Jesus was pure and blameless. He had an actual human body with human emotions and thoughts, yet He lived with purity and self-sacrifice. Because of Him, we know what a human life filled with shalom, with flourishing, looks like.

This time of year offers us a lot of ideas of what it means to flourish. Think of all the commercials and Christmas-themed romantic comedies. What is the world's or culture's definition of *holistic flourishing*?

Deepest shalom is found in living a life that pleases the God of peace, in imitation of Jesus Christ. Because of His death and resurrection, this is actually possible by the work of His Spirit. Paul prayed this over a group of believers two thousand years ago, so let's borrow this prayer for ourselves and those around us.

God of shalom, only in You is found deep, holistic, human flourishing. As Creator and King, Your rule, Your presence, and Your way of life are truly beautiful and the only way for me to live fully human. If there's any part of my spirit, soul, or body that isn't submitted to Your kingship, please reveal it to me. Continue Your sanctifying work in me, Lord.

Pray the blessing of 1 Thessalonians 5:23–24 over someone today. Consider doing this even for someone you don't know well. If someone crosses your path and seems to be in need of encouragement or strength, just ask if you can pray a blessing over them that's been on your mind. You may be surprised at their yes! Or send a Christmas card to someone with this as the blessing on the card.

DAY 7

INSTRUCTIONS WHILE IN EXILE

 Glance through your calendar for the coming day or week. Very practically speaking, what work are you doing? Are you driving kids around, typing away in a cubicle, folding laundry, nursing a baby, breaking a sweat working outside or in a room full of students or patients or customers? Pay attention to any feelings that arise as you think about your schedule.

> This is what the LORD Almighty, the God of Israel, says to all those I carried into exile from Jerusalem to Babylon: "Build houses and settle down; plant gardens and eat what they produce. Marry and have sons and daughters; find wives for your sons and give your daughters in marriage, so that they too may have sons and daughters. Increase in number there; do not decrease. Also, seek the peace and prosperity of the city to which I have carried you into exile. Pray to the LORD for it, because if it prospers, you too will prosper."
>
> Jeremiah 29:4–7

In a sense, we're living in exile. All around us is a broken world with a culture and way of life that's antithetical to the kingdom of Jesus, with so many opportunities to forget and even forsake a life of following Jesus and living His Beautiful Way.

This passage of Scripture is a message from God through the prophet Jeremiah to His people as they're in exile in the pagan nation of Babylon. They struggled to know how to walk with God intimately when all around them were reasons not to. Does this feel relatable? When there's an easier way to live right before us, it's almost impossible to resist. But we get to listen in and see if there's anything for us in these words.

From the passage, how would you summarize God's to-do list for these exiles thousands of years ago?

It's incredible to notice that this is an echo of the to-do list for human beings in the creation account in the book of Genesis. There it says that God placed the man and woman in the garden to care for it, maintain it, and eat freely from it. The man and woman were also made to reproduce and flourish and increase in number. "Be fruitful and multiply! Fill the earth and subdue it!" (Genesis 1:28 NET). The garden of Eden was a far cry from exile in Babylon, and some things had really changed, but God reminded the people that some things had *not* changed.

Our life today is extremely complicated, but what a grounding truth that some things haven't changed. There's still work to be done. There are still things to create in partnership with God. He still desires for us to work together with Him for the good of the world.

What in your life does this simple truth speak to today? What is your work in your corner of the world today?

This message through the prophet Jeremiah has something else for those who live in exile. It says in verse 7, "Seek the peace and prosperity of the city to which I have carried you into exile. Pray to the Lord for it." In the midst of hardship, godless practices, and possible mistreatment, we aren't encouraged to just keep our heads down and do our work and mind our business, though that would be easier. We're called to pursue the peace, or shalom, of the city we're in.

The call isn't just to work for self and family but to work and pray for the flourishing of the people around you. The people you may not agree with or understand.

God, right now I pause to pray for those who dwell in the corner of the world You've brought me to. Because of the challenges and complexity of life, because of mere fatigue, it's easy to want to hunker down and mind my own business. To worry about just me and those belonging to me. But I hear Your invitation to look around. May Your blessing and favor and peace be on the people in my neighborhood, the people in my workplace, the people in my child(ren)'s school, the people in my local grocery store. Would You show me a small step to take to bring flourishing to one of them today?

Take a walk through your neighborhood or a nearby park without music or a podcast, without texting. Maybe just keep your phone in your pocket! Look and notice *with Jesus* the people around you. Pray for them. Make eye contact and smile. Can you even on your walk bring a small bit of flourishing to your city with a kind greeting, by petting a dog, or by picking up some trash?

WE HAVE JOY

REJOICE, HE IS NEAR

Pour yourself a drink with carbonation, with fizz. A soda, ginger ale, sparkling water, kombucha. As you taste the texture the bubbles add to your beverage, reflect on any creative connection between this experience and the word *rejoice*.

> Rejoice in the Lord always. I will say it again: Rejoice! Let your gentleness be evident to all. The Lord is near.
>
> Philippians 4:4–5

Who is someone special to you—someone you may not get to see often?

There's something special about being near the people who mean the most to us. When we're children, they might be our parents or grandparents, aunts or uncles. As we grow, they become our school-age friends and significant others. And then as we enter adulthood and have children of our own, the special people in life include our children and grandchildren. And soon we realize the importance of soaking up every single moment with them, because those moments feel rare and fleeting.

Isn't it strange how the importance of being around those we love—though always something we seek and cherish—becomes more and more apparent with each passing year? The older we get, the more we realize how precious these relationships are. We were made to be with people.

As you think on the joy you feel being in the presence of your dearest loved ones, I want you to think about being in the presence of Jesus, God incarnate. Imagine Him walking into the room, greeting you with a hug, taking a seat beside you, asking about your day. Imagine the joy and awe.

When you think of Jesus being with you right now, what do you imagine or envision?

The disciples lived this. They ate with Him, slept near Him, and walked beside Him mile after mile. They likely argued with Him and may have even become frustrated with Him when His ways didn't line up with their broken desires. Yet they remained near to Him and He to them.

How incredible that experience must've been! While it may be easy to think of them as lucky, the truth is that God is near, God is here, even now.

As you sit and read this book, Jesus is near.

As you go about your day, Jesus is near.

As you make mistakes and strain to hear His voice, Jesus is near.

He isn't an occasional presence or a family member we only see a few times a year. Our time with Him isn't limited, and our days with Him aren't numbered.

He is near, just as Philippians 4:4–5 states. And that truth should bring overwhelming joy—the joy of a Lord who is with us.

As we enter this third week of Advent, let's bask in the joy that is our Savior.

Lord, I sit in Your presence right now, and I invite You to be close. To make Your presence known. To remind me that You're here with me, even when things don't go according to plan. Even when I'm stuck in the monotony of work or parenting or responsibilities. And You're here with me when I experience breakthrough. When I'm overjoyed. When I follow You in word and deed. You are near. You are here. Thank You. Help me to never take that for granted.

Use your phone to set reminders throughout the day at random intervals. Each time the alarm goes off, take a moment to let it sink in. Jesus is near. Jesus is here. And what does His nearness compel you to do? Worship? Pray? Bow? Converse? Serve? Listen and then do, just as you would if your favorite person showed up at your doorstep. You'd be compelled to action. Let it be so.

THE PRESENCE OF GOD

 Light a candle. Think of the flame as a representation of the presence of Jesus Christ, who is with you in this very moment.

Preserve me, O God, for in you I take refuge.
I say to the Lord, "You are my Lord;
    I have no good apart from you."

As for the saints in the land, they are the excellent ones,
    in whom is all my delight.

The sorrows of those who run after another god shall
        multiply;
    their drink offerings of blood I will not pour out
    or take their names on my lips.

The Lord is my chosen portion and my cup;
    you hold my lot.
The lines have fallen for me in pleasant places;
    indeed, I have a beautiful inheritance.

I bless the Lord who gives me counsel;
    in the night also my heart instructs me.
I have set the Lord always before me;
    because he is at my right hand, I shall not be
        shaken.

Therefore my heart is glad, and my whole being
        rejoices;

my flesh also dwells secure.
  For you will not abandon my soul to Sheol,
      or let your holy one see corruption.

You make known to me the path of life;
      in your presence there is fullness of joy;
      at your right hand are pleasures forevermore.

Psalm 16 ESV

What brings you joy lately? What gets you jumping out of bed in the morning, eager to start the day? What has you praising and thanking God? Is it a relationship? An opportunity? A favorite spot on the back porch or a much-anticipated event? A trip to the gym or a new toy?

Life can be beautiful, and we were made to enjoy it! But unless our joy is rooted in the King, it won't last.

The relationship will hit a bump. The opportunity will take a turn. The fun event or moment of solitude will come and go. The gym won't always fit into the day's schedule. The new toy will get old. And what then? What happens when the thing that brings joy no longer fills that need?

Reflect back on Psalm 16 and take note of where believers can and can't find joy:

Psalm 16 makes many important statements, but there are two overarching themes. First, the presence of God—spending time with Him in prayer and Scripture reading—brings *fullness* of joy. Second, the gods of this world—the things we do, seek, and idolize in place of God—bring sorrow.

Consider those truths for a moment, and if you can, write down three things that pull you away from prayer and Scripture reading (such as television, social media, a busy calendar, overtime at work, hobbies, etc.). Indicate how much time you give to each one every week.

Now give a rough estimate of how much intentional time you spend focused on God and in communion with other believers every week.

The presence of God is a game changer. It's a difference maker in our lives. It literally brings fullness of joy . . . yet many times prayer and Scripture reading and community with other believers get the least amount of our attention.

A common platitude for the Jesus follower is to find joy in the hope of salvation—joy in the knowledge that this life isn't the end. Psalm 16 touches a bit on this, but in no way is the life to come the beginning and end of our joy. Verse 11 is clear. Joy comes by being in the presence of God. And it's available *now*.

What would happen if Jesus followers lived this? What would happen if we prioritized presence with God and lived our lives with the acute awareness that He is with us and His hand is on our lives *today*?

This joy is powerful, because not only does it point to our eternal hope, but it also reveals the incredible importance of now.

Yes, we have joy because of the salvation found through Jesus Christ. We have joy in the knowledge that He will reconcile the world and make all things right—Advent is a reminder of this! And we *also* have joy in the knowledge that our day-to-day, Christ-filled life—the comings and goings, the ordinary and extraordinary—are infused with His presence if only we take the time to see. If only we pull away from the gods of this world and devote more of our lives to seeking His presence.

> *Lord, I offer to You my striving and desire for the things of this world that pull my attention away from Your presence. Convict me in this, Lord. Show me the areas I haven't yet given over to You. And meet me in my desire to be in Your presence more and more each day.*

Take a string and tie it around your wrist. For the rest of the day or week, when you look at that string, consider that God is with you and that He's inviting you to experience His presence. Respond to those promptings as you feel led in the moment.

JOYFUL FAITHFULNESS

 If weather permits, go outside or sit by a window where there's plenty of sunlight. Let the sun warm your skin. Let the breeze, whether cool or warm, move over your face and breathe life into you. Maybe lift your hands as a symbol of worship. Even if you don't feel joyful, take a moment to think about joy and the times when your joy has been abundant. Think about the joy we have in the Lord.

> Though the fig tree does not bud
>   and there are no grapes on the vines,
> though the olive crop fails
>   and the fields produce no food,
> though there are no sheep in the pen
>   and no cattle in the stalls,
> yet I will rejoice in the LORD,
>   I will be joyful in God my Savior.
>
> The Sovereign LORD is my strength;
>   he makes my feet like the feet of a deer,
>   he enables me to tread on the heights.
>
> Habakkuk 3:17–19

It's thought that the prophet Habakkuk wrote his namesake book when the Babylonians overtook Jerusalem. The Babylonians were brutal and unforgiving and pagan, and Habakkuk had to trust his God in the face of inevitable persecution and hardship. All seemed lost.

With this in mind, it's no wonder he wrote this pained, heartfelt book. In it, he challenges God, asking Him why bad things happen to God's faithful people. Yet despite his anguish, Habakkuk does what's so very hard to do—he remains not only faithful but overjoyed in his faith.

Imagine being so deeply trusting and intimate with God that even the presence of your enemy on your doorstep doesn't remove your joy! This is the depth of relationship available to us.

Read Psalm 33 from the perspective of finding joy in the Lord and trusting in Him no matter what. What stands out to you?

Joy is so different than happiness. Happiness comes and goes, but joy is a deep contentment and satisfaction that can't be shaken. It's a reflection of our faith—of our ability (or lack of ability) to lay our concerns and fears at the altar. And it's from this truth that we rejoice. Even when we receive a disheartening phone call or are shattered after a broken relationship. Even when the business fails and the bank account is drained. Even when those we love turn against us and slander our name. We can have joy because we have faith. The sovereign Lord is our strength. He enables us to "tread on the heights," as Habakkuk so eloquently shared.

Consider the times when you've felt joy in hardship. What was that like?

Take a moment to think about your relationship with God. What emotions does it bring up within you? Is joy one of them?

God of Habakkuk, You offer the same joy to me that You provided to him. I praise You for this gift, and I humbly ask that You help me to accept it fully. Help me to sense that deep, inner joy You bring even in my sorrow, confusion, frustration, and exhaustion.

There's power in words and in our mindset. When you feel your joy dying out, pause and contemplate the joy found in the Lord. Repeat the phrases from Habakkuk aloud: "I will rejoice in the LORD, I will be joyful in God my Savior." If these words were powerful enough to keep Habakkuk's heart in tune with God even in the midst of wartime devastation, then they're certainly powerful enough for us.

IF NOTHING ELSE, CHOOSE TO ABIDE

Choose your favorite place to relax in your home. That spot you always go to put up your feet. Sit or lie in that place. When do you tend to go to this place? How much time have you spent simply *being there*? Take some breaths and notice how your body relaxes and softens here.

> If you keep my commands, you will remain in my love, just as I have kept my Father's commands and remain in his love. I have told you this so that my joy may be in you and that your joy may be complete.
>
> John 15:10–11

When do you feel joy the most? When do you feel it the least? Can you identify patterns?

Daily joy can be a struggle. It's easy to be joyful when God moves the mountains in our midst or when His presence is strongly felt. But day-in, day-out joy? That can seem distant and unobtainable, yet as John 15:10–11 shows, complete joy is possible. How can this be? Where does this joy come from? Sure, we know it comes from God, but *how do we fully receive it?*

Read John 15:10–12 again. Jesus tells us that joy comes from remaining—or abiding—in Him. When we abide in Him, we're able to fully receive His love and live in that complete joy because that is the essence of who He is!

There's a challenge in this passage as well. To abide in Him, we must keep His commandments. But John wasn't simply referring to a checklist of dos and don'ts. As Jesus explained, the greatest commandment—the commandment that's most important—is to truly love God (Matthew 22:36–40). Orient your life toward loving God and everything else falls into place.

To love Him is to seek after Him. It's to commune with Him, worship Him. To cling to Him—not just to follow Him. And the beginning and end of this is to *abide.*

When did you last spend time trying to abide in Christ? Take a moment and do that now. Open your hands and heart and tell Jesus that you're resting, abiding in Him today.

It's the softened posture of abiding in King Jesus in the present that allows us to receive the love that God has for us at every moment. Which in turn makes us more loving. And this leads to us experiencing complete joy.

Lord, You love me just as I am. And even now with all my shortcomings, You offer me Your good and perfect love. Open my eyes to the ways that I can soften my heart toward You. Show me Your kingdom way of life. Help me to lean into this and experience the complete joy that comes from knowing and abiding in You.

As you go about your daily tasks, consider how King Jesus may be inviting you into a more missional way of life as you abide in Him and receive more of His love and joy. What might that look like for you? Does it mean spending more time with your neighbors? Inviting people over regularly for dinner? Volunteering for that cause you feel passionately about? Leading a group of believers? Identify this next step and take action.

WHEN SORROWS LIKE SEA BILLOWS ROLL

 Light a candle and think of something you long for. Perhaps a mended relationship? Full health for a loved one? A reprieve from the pain of the past? A day away from the chaos of life? Now spend time praying aloud, worshiping and praising God. Notice the sound of your heartfelt pleas as you verbally acknowledge and give that thing to the Holy Spirit.

> Therefore you now have sorrow; but I will see you again and your heart will rejoice, and your joy no one will take from you.
>
> John 16:22 NKJV

Here's what we tend to get wrong about joy: a joyful life doesn't mean a life free of sorrow or grief or longing.

In John 16, Jesus is in the midst of saying farewell to His disciples. It's the night before His crucifixion, and He is preparing them for what's about to happen (His death and resurrection) while also laying a foundation for the church to come.

He shares an analogy of a woman giving birth. Jesus is clear that labor is difficult but that mothers are overcome with joy when they hold their baby in their arms. Likewise, the disciples are about to go through incredible sorrow and pain as Jesus will be tortured and crucified. But their joy will be immeasurable upon His resurrection!

In this seemingly dichotomous relationship between sorrow and joy, it's important to see that Jesus makes room for sadness and grief, and yet He is always joyful. At no point does He condemn those more difficult and uncomfortable feelings. Rather, He acknowledges them, making it clear that they're only natural. He also shows us that it's possible—and even right—to hold both sorrow and joy at once.

How do you hold sorrow? What does it look like in your life? Do you make space for it?

We Jesus followers may be sorrowful at the brokenness in this world, yet we're hopeful in God's perfect plan. As we sit in our sorrow, it's important to believe this. It's important to know that grief and longing are part of being human. It's how we were created! It's unhealthy for us to push our feelings aside or to make one another feel guilty for the sadness we feel.

How did Jesus handle grief in John 11?

We don't have to apologize for our grief or sorrow—but we also don't have to allow it to shift our attention away from Christ. May we grieve with kingdom focus. May our sorrow be rooted in the hope we have in Him. May our anguish cling to the love and joy He offers— joy that can never be taken from us. As Horatio Spafford's powerful hymn describes:

> When peace like a river attendeth my way,
> When sorrows like sea billows roll;
> Whatever my lot, Thou hast taught me to say,
> "It is well, it is well with my soul."

Father, You are with me in my sorrow and grief. You understand and see me, and You'll sit with me in this for as long as I need. You aren't in a rush. You aren't urging me to get over it. You created me to grieve, to feel sadness, to react when the brokenness of this world is too much. Yet You offer a joy that can't be taken away. Help me to feel that joy. Help me to see it. Help me to live a life that exists in that complexity of sorrow over a broken world and incredible joy that changes everything.

When you come across something that brings sorrow or sadness today, pause. Take a moment to allow yourself to sit in that feeling while being aware that deep joy is always available to you in Jesus. Think through the dichotomy of the two. Then share that sorrow with a brother or sister in Christ. Do that today.

DO THE THING

Pull out your holiday to-do list. This could include gifts you need to buy, things you need to do, food you need to prepare. (If you don't have a list, spend some time writing things down.) Find a scent that grounds you—an oil from the cabinet, an herb from the baking cupboard. Consider these good and meaningful plans you're holding in your heart—plans to make this holiday season important and memorable for others—as you breathe in that focus-giving scent.

> Each of you should give what you have decided in your heart to give, not reluctantly or under compulsion, for God loves a cheerful giver. And God is able to bless you abundantly, so that in all things at all times, having all that you need, you will abound in every good work. . . .
>
> This service that you perform is not only supplying the needs of the Lord's people but is also overflowing in many expressions of thanks to God.
>
> 2 Corinthians 9:7–8, 12

Christmas is right around the corner, and this is the time of year when we may find our emotions vacillating between two extremes. The first is an indescribable joy and anticipation for the holiday season and everything it brings—family, meals together at the table, time spent intentionally with loved ones. In this, we joyfully make to-do lists and eagerly await seeing those plans come through.

The second extreme we may feel is much less desirable. We think about ourselves. We feel sorry for ourselves and all that we have done or are doing that goes unnoticed. Unthanked. Unreciprocated. We look at all the effort we've put toward making this season memorable for others—the decorations, the financial expense, the giving of our time and home—and we view ourselves as having sacrificed it all . . . and gotten nothing in return.

In these moments, our joy is gone. What began as a way for us to show love to others becomes a dangerous mental spiral that puts us right where the Enemy wants us.

How is your joy threatened when it comes to planning and executing holiday goals?

Second Corinthians 9 speaks exactly to this heart posture of self-pity and disappointment. Notice how plainly it states, "Each of you should give what you have decided in your heart to give" (v. 7). So those times that we think of good ways to show love to others? The Bible tells us to do the thing regardless of whether it's reciprocated. When our hearts move, give that donation. Shovel that neighbor's driveway. Put up the Christmas tree, making it fun for the kids. Prepare that holiday feast that others will eat.

Do the thing. Without waiting for or needing appreciation and admiration. Do the thing. And let the fact that you're giving to others flood you with joy and cheer, overflowing in expressions of thanks to God. You see, it's through our joyful *doing* that we show God gratitude in a way that's multilayered, multifaceted, and heartfelt.

Think about something you want to do for someone else this holiday season. What is the reaction you're hoping for?

Now take a breath. Picture getting no recognition or praise for doing that thing—and then imagine the worship God receives in your offering. Write your thoughts here.

Joy in loving others brings about abundance and gratitude to God. Few things in this broken life are so immediately rewarding spiritually and mentally. Let this holiday season be the start of a more intentional awareness of how what we do matters to Him. Let us cast aside selfish motives and expectations and realize that it's not about us. It's about Him, and He multiplies every good deed.

> *Father, I'm looking again at this list I made of good things I want to do for others. I'm deciding to do these things joyfully, knowing that You bring abundance through my efforts and that in my cheerfulness I show You gratitude. Help me to remember this. When I feel my selfishness creep in, help me to repeat, "I'm giving what God has put on my heart to give."*

Is there a good work you've avoided doing for fear that it would be too difficult, too much of a sacrifice, or too likely to go unnoticed? Follow through now with a cheerful heart. Get friends to help if you need more hands. Then be sensitive to how God may move or speak in your life as a result of doing the thing.

ENJOYMENT IN THE NOW

 Taste a piece of fruit. Notice the complexity of flavor and texture. The natural sweetness and tanginess. Consider what a blessing it is to enjoy God's provision in this way.

> Behold, what I have seen to be good and fitting is to eat and drink and find enjoyment in all the toil with which one toils under the sun the few days of his life that God has given him, for this is his lot. Everyone also to whom God has given wealth and possessions and power to enjoy them, and to accept his lot and rejoice in his toil—this is the gift of God. For he will not much remember the days of his life because God keeps him occupied with joy in his heart.
>
> Ecclesiastes 5:18–20 ESV

What does your life look like? *Really*, what does it look like? What are your responsibilities and tasks? What do you do for a living and where do you live? What does your earthly wealth look like? Write it all out here.

Now take a breath. How do you feel about all of this? Are you content with your life as it is or are you searching for something else?

For many of us, true contentment feels like an impossible goal. We live in a culture that champions year-over-year success and growth. We ditch our friends when they aren't being friendly enough and our jobs when they aren't paying enough. We think nothing of cutting ties and moving on to the next thing in hopes that it will get us to where we want to go.

And the big casualty in all of this is our joy.

Ecclesiastes 5:18–20 spells it out plainly. Joy comes with acceptance. To rejoice in the work of our hands, we have to accept the work as it is. To rejoice in the provisions given to us, we have to accept those provisions as they are. To rejoice in the day before us, we have to accept it as it is.

The author of Ecclesiastes knew that the best is never good enough.

The top is never high enough. A bigger house is never big enough. A more powerful position is never powerful enough . . .

Not until we accept our lives as they are today. Now, this doesn't mean we entirely leave ambition at the door. We were made to be fruitful and multiply! But if we're always looking for what's next instead of enjoying what is before us, then we're missing out on the joy of the Lord.

What is standing in the way of you accepting the life you've been given? Is it your desire to succeed? To achieve a certain standard of living? To keep up with everyone else?

What step might you take today to remove that thing that's standing in the way?

Let this be your excuse today and every day to be happy with what you have, however much or little. To laugh loudly. Love deeply. Live passionately. And be content with things as they are. Do this, and watch God swoop in with the gift of a joyful heart.

Lord, I confess my discontent, my striving for things, money, notoriety, a certain standard of living that's clouded my view. I confess this and I ask that You do a work in me. Tear down those expectations I've built. Help me to drink, eat, and live in complete acceptance of what You've provided this day.

Take money you've been setting aside—money you've been intending to use in an effort to buy contentment—and pray over it. Ask God how He wants you to use the money. Does He want you to donate it? Buy gifts for a needy family? Spend the money on a family getaway? Pay off debt? Ask for His guidance, and follow through.

✦ Week Four of Advent ✦

WE HAVE LOVE

A MORE PERFECT LOVE

👁 Look at a picture of someone you deeply love. A child. A parent. A spouse. A friend. Spend some moments really thinking of your depth of love for that person.

> Dear friends, let us love one another, for love comes from God. Everyone who loves has been born of God and knows God. Whoever does not love does not know God, because God is love.
>
> 1 John 4:7–8

Perfect love comes from God.

We've heard this many times and probably even believe it whole-heartedly. But when was the last time you truly thought about all of the ways that human love is imperfect while God's love is complete?

No matter how hard I try to show love and be love, I still end up hurting the people who mean the most to me. I make rude comments or act selfishly. I put my needs first, and instead of denying myself I deny the ones I love. I hold grudges, struggle with forgiveness, and fail over and over to meet their needs without strings attached.

With such a bad track record of loving others, it can be hard to imagine—truly imagine!—a perfect love.

If someone were to love you perfectly, what would that look like?

Imagine a love that's always there, that never runs out, that always forgives, always welcomes back, always works to *show* itself.

And then imagine a love so perfect and so strong that it causes us to love others more completely! That's exactly what Jesus offers. He offers us perfect love that spills out to those around us.

Are you claiming this today? Are you accepting His perfect love and allowing it to move through you and out to others?

It's such a simple concept, but it's the light and life of the hope we have here on earth. To better love those around us, we need more Jesus.

This is the reason He came. To show love and be love. It's the thrust of this final week of Advent and the culmination of the season. Everything—gratitude, hope, peace, joy—is meaningless without love. And our efforts to love outside of Him fall short. Let's remember this as we press into this week with intentionality.

Heavenly Father, I recognize that love begins and ends with You. Apart from You, we're broken humans trying to achieve the unachievable. And with You, we have an opportunity to love others in ways that could leave them speechless. We have an opportunity to love others with a more perfect, more beautiful love. Help me to exercise that love today and every day. Keep me by Your side so that I may always choose the love You offer and pour it out onto others.

Spend time in prayer today and ask God for two things. Ask Him to show you His love for you. And then ask Him to help you show greater love to someone in your life. Write down what happens in your heart and mind as a result.

Sense of Wonder

AN UNCONDITIONAL BLESSING

Find a scent in your house that smells clean. (Isn't it funny that certain scents make us think certain things?) It could be a candle, an oil, a body lotion, a soap. Take some moments to close your eyes and breathe it in. Wash your hands in it if that makes sense to do. Imagine a fresh start—whatever that may look like for you.

> The LORD did not set his affection on you and choose you because you were more numerous than other peoples, for you were the fewest of all peoples. But it was because the LORD loved you and kept the oath he swore to your ancestors that he brought you out with a mighty hand and redeemed you from the land of slavery, from the power of Pharaoh king of Egypt. Know therefore that the LORD your God is God; he is the faithful God, keeping his covenant of love to a thousand generations of those who love him and keep his commandments.
>
> Deuteronomy 7:7–9

God's love is perfect. And it's perfect because it's *unconditional*. It's a covenant love, as the Deuteronomy passage states. He is bound to it!

When it comes to God's love, there's no riddle to solve or password to utter at the gate. No strings attached, no expectation on His part.

He loves us all the time, no matter what, and He's constantly extending that love toward us.

He loves us knowing that we'll slip up, that we'll fall short. He loves us knowing that we won't ever be able to pay Him back or even begin to reciprocate what He so freely offers us. And He chooses to love us anyway, day after day.

If you ever need a reminder of exactly how forgiving and unconditional God's love is, think of the story of Israel. How quickly they forgot His love! How quickly they forgot their captivity in Egypt and how God parted the Red Sea so they would be saved. How quickly they forgot the provision of manna and the cloud that guided them by day and the fire that guided them by night. Over and over they forgot about God's love. And over and over He welcomed them back.

The same can be said for us. How quickly we forget the depth of God's love. How quickly we turn to idols—things we think will satisfy and bring us what we want. And how steady is His call to us, bringing us back.

What are some things in your life you chase after because you believe they'll make you happier? (Some ideas include money, relationships, fame, possessions, experiences, independence, education, etc.)

In what ways have you forgotten all that the Lord has done in your life?

Deuteronomy 7:7–9 says it so beautifully. We've done nothing to earn or keep His love, yet He offers it to us anyway. Within His love we find redemption and freedom and power—not only for us but for a thousand generations to come if we so choose.

God's love is a love that's always available. Always offered free of charge for us and all the generations to come after us. All He asks is that we receive it and live within it.

How are you choosing to live within God's love today?

What might the future look like if you walk in God's love and if God's favor passes to your children and grandchildren and so on? What would that kind of legacy mean to you?

God's perfect, unconditional love is available for us today. Even if we're not feeling up to it. Even if things have gone wrong. Even if we're struggling with an idol or two. He wants us to choose His love and let Him do a work in us. Won't you let Him work?

Father, no one loves like You. No one forgives like You, forgets like You, looks past my brokenness the way You do. I'm so unworthy—so very unworthy—yet You offer me life-changing love. Love that can impact the world. Love that can impact generations to come. This no-strings-attached love is what I so desperately choose today. Help me to stay centered in it and to do all things through it and through Your power today and every day. Amen.

Listen to "The Blessing" by Elevation Worship and Kari Jobe. (There's a video of it on YouTube.) Think back and remember God's faithful love to you. What has He done in your life through the years? Make a list or journal out these small and big signs of His covenant love to you.

LOVE SEES

Find something that someone made for you: a blanket, a painting, a winter hat. Hold it in your hands. Consider the time and effort—the love—*that went into creating the gift, and how the act of giving it to you was such a small part of the beautiful process of someone seeing you and wanting to show you love in a unique way.*

> Jesus went through all the towns and villages, teaching in their synagogues, proclaiming the good news of the kingdom and healing every disease and sickness. When he saw the crowds, he had compassion on them, because they were harassed and helpless, like sheep without a shepherd.
>
> Matthew 9:35–36

It's mind-blowing that the thing that gave purpose to Jesus's time on earth and changed the future of the world wasn't just His singular, mighty act of love on the cross. *It was also the life of love He lived every day.*

This is something we tend to miss. We zoom in on the cross and the resurrection, which brought incredible hope and beauty and meaning to life . . . and we forget that all of it was built on year after year of Jesus loving and seeing the people around Him.

Jesus wasn't a God-man who rose up out of nowhere to do what needed to be done at the right time and in the right place at Calvary. The cross wasn't the beginning and end of Jesus's purpose here on earth. No. Jesus was a servant of love. He loved constantly and completely. And His love led Him to the cross. Jesus's death wouldn't have had the same impact if He hadn't backed up His sacrifice with years and years of loving people well.

Journal your thoughts about the reality that it was *because* of Jesus's life of love that the cross was meaningful (and not the other way around!).

Jesus loved so well in His daily life because *He saw people.* He took the time to notice them. To think compassionately about them. And He did this everywhere He went. "Sheep without a shepherd," He called them in Matthew 9:36. He saw people striving, wandering, struggling, searching, looking for answers and a place to belong and coming up empty-handed.

He saw this. And He was moved by it.

When was the last time we truly saw the people around us? When was the last time we focused more on what's right in front of us and less on the big, flashy things we've got planned for the future?

How do you see people?

What needs to change?

Jesus, Your life of love is evident throughout the Gospels. You were honest, kind, and merciful toward all, and You showed us the power and effectiveness of that approach. Lord, I see the fullness of Your message. I see how Your life wasn't just about the cross but also about how You lived. Help me to remember this! Help me to move more and more toward a posture of daily love for others, no matter our differences. No matter what others may think. No matter the pressure I may face to take a different approach. Help me to see others clearly but also with great compassion, just like You did.

Think of a person in your life who you struggle to have compassion and love for. This man or woman, this child, could even live in your house. Jesus sees that person too and is able to shift your gaze. Today, take a step toward changing the way you see and treat that friend or family member or coworker. Write a kind note, give a compliment, bring over a meal, or make eye contact and smile. Do something to train yourself to see with compassion and act with love, because it is your life of love that punctuates your legacy.

HOW IS YOUR LOVE?

Play an audio recording of someone you love. Close your eyes and listen to the sound of his or her voice. Let yourself feel the love you have for that person.

> If I speak in the tongues of men or of angels, but do not have love, I am only a resounding gong or a clanging cymbal. If I have the gift of prophecy and can fathom all mysteries and all knowledge, and if I have a faith that can move mountains, but do not have love, I am nothing. If I give all I possess to the poor and give over my body to hardship that I may boast, but do not have love, I gain nothing.
>
> 1 Corinthians 13:1–3

Love is something Jesus followers are to be known for (John 13:35), yet many outside of the church don't view us in that way.

We speak proudly, confidently. We push our opinions, our yard signs, our ministries, our giftings, our political stances, and our talking heads, insisting that we have everything figured out. We insist that we're right, that we're compassionate, that we're smart—and yet we have forgotten to love.

Let's absorb more of Paul's words to the Corinthians in this treatise on love.

> Love is patient, love is kind. It does not envy, it does not boast, it is not proud. It does not dishonor others,

it is not self-seeking, it is not easily angered, it keeps no record of wrongs. Love does not delight in evil but rejoices with the truth. It always protects, always trusts, always hopes, always perseveres.

Love never fails. But where there are prophecies, they will cease; where there are tongues, they will be stilled; where there is knowledge, it will pass away. (1 Corinthians 13:4–8)

When you read this, what does it do to you? Do you find a "yeah, but . . ." on the tip of your tongue as your mind flashes to all the people in your life who are hard to love? Or is your heart stirred to action?

What are some of your excuses or "yeah, buts" to this passage? Be honest and list them.

Now that you've had a moment of self-reflection, think about how God has gifted you to love. Consider each statement in the above verses. What are some ways you naturally love others well?

How is God inviting you to grow in love based on this passage?

This lifestyle of love is the most important witness we have, because it's not through our opinions or beliefs or Facebook posts that people are pointed to Jesus; it's through our love. Love cuts through the noise of this world that's telling everyone to think about themselves, to take care of themselves, to do what's best for themselves.

It's our love that shows we truly believe in Jesus.

Friend, how is your love?

Is it patient?

Is it kind?

Is it content?

Is it humble?

Does it lift up others?

Does it offer others a clean slate every single day?

Does it rejoice in truth?

Does it protect, trust, hope, persevere?

Does it remain steadfast even when it feels like you're tearing your heart apart loving someone who has such a hard time accepting it?

Friend, how is your love? And how is Jesus calling you to go deeper?

Jesus, I see how You were and are patient, kind, content, humble, uplifting, forgiving—a truth teller, a protector, a confidant, a proponent of hope and perseverance. I see how You were steadfast in Your love, even when people were mocking You. Even as they crucified You. Show me how I can be more like You. Show me my selfishness. Break it all apart for more of You.

Where is your love for others lacking? Is it in your responses to others, your ability to have compassion, your patience with others' flaws? Be honest about this with God and ask Him to show you how to be more loving in those situations. How can you, when it really counts—which means when it's really hard— be gentler, more patient, kinder, and so on? Try it today.

ATTACHMENT LOVE

Steep a cup of tea. Choose a tea bag or gather loose leaves while water boils. As you submerge the dried leaves, watch the water change color, feel the steam rise from the mug, and then patiently wait for the infusion to cool enough to drink. Sip the tea. Think about how chewing the raw leaves would be too intense and bitter and gritty, but in boiled water the leaves become nuanced. The water takes on flavor that is soothing and comforting, with properties that can be healing.

When Israel was a child, I loved him,
    and out of Egypt I called my son.
But the more they were called,
    the more they went away from me.
They sacrificed to the Baals
    and they burned incense to images.
It was I who taught Ephraim to walk,
    taking them by the arms;
but they did not realize
    it was I who healed them.
I led them with cords of human kindness,
    with ties of love.
To them I was like one who lifts
    a little child to the cheek,
    and I bent down to feed them.

Hosea 11:1–4

In its healthiest and purest sense, a mother's love is fierce and unconditional. God designed the attachment bond between mother and child to be nurturing and formative from the very start. The moment every child enters the world, God deems that life so beautiful and precious that it's worth the complete devotion of another human being (a mother). This love is unique among all other loves and relationships. This love keeps the mother awake at night praying. It compels her to persevere through sleeplessness and sacrifice.

Ideally, the mother is accepting of this responsibility, equipped with resources and abilities, and fully invested in the health and well-being of the child. We know in this broken world that isn't always the case, and this is something to grieve. Maybe you had a mother who was attentive and compassionate; maybe you didn't. This is the profound truth: you are worthy of the maternal, nurturing love of a mother. And even the best earthly motherly love is only a reflection of God's tender love toward us.

Because of the picture we see so often this time of year of the baby Jesus and his mother Mary, it's appropriate that we remember that God doesn't love just like a Father, but He loves like a mother. A mother's love sees the best and forgives the worst. A mother never gives up. A mother welcomes back with open arms. Like Hosea 11 states, motherly love calls by name, teaches, lifts up, leads, draws close, and feeds. A mother loves with her actions.

What was your mother's love like?

Pause for a moment and picture the love described in Hosea 11 as God's love for you. What feelings or doubts or questions arise?

If Jesus embodies this maternal love for the world and invites us to love like Him, what if we approached the hurting people around us with this type of love? What if we saw others—even those we've identified as hard to love—as people who God has placed in our lives so we can show them active love? Like children without a mother, like sheep without a shepherd.

Consider the people in your life (outside of your family) who you naturally tend to show active love toward the most. What do those people look like? How do they act? How do they think, vote, live?

Are there others around you who are harder to love, who are hurting, who are different than you, who could really use the nurturing love of God expressed through you? Who are they and how could you love them today?

Just like in the passage, sometimes a child strays. Sometimes a hurting person, like a wounded animal, resists love and pushes away affection and care. What if we sought out these people in our midst instead of getting exasperated and giving up? What if we pursued those who are different from us? What if we chased after them with the same active love a mother has for her child? And maybe hardest of all, what if we received the maternal, nurturing, unconditional love the creator God has for us right now?

Jesus, I see Your perfect love in the love of a mother. How she's quick to offer help and comfort and guidance. How her door is always open to welcome back a wayward child.

How she doesn't judge and doesn't expect anything in return.
Help me to see that this kind of love isn't just for a mother
and her children. It's for all of us as we love those around
us. I pray that You give me an active, lively love today for
those around me and that I see them the way You see them.

Think about someone you've written off as "too difficult to love," who you "just don't get along" with. What can you do today to show active love toward that person? What can you do tomorrow? Spend a few moments thinking about how you can show love to this person more and more every day.

A LOVE WORTH FIGHTING FOR

Think about a task you want to do for someone who is not relationally close to you. Perhaps you've thought about raking your neighbor's leaves or writing an encouraging email to someone you know only in passing. Close your eyes and allow yourself to feel whatever this stirs within you: excitement, nervousness, hesitancy, hopefulness.

> "The most important one," answered Jesus, "is this: 'Hear, O Israel: The Lord our God, the Lord is one. Love the Lord your God with all your heart and with all your soul and with all your mind and with all your strength.' The second is this: 'Love your neighbor as yourself.' There is no commandment greater than these."
>
> Mark 12:29–31

Mark 12:29–31 tells us to love God with everything we have and then to spill that love over onto others. This twofold command to love God and to love people is the greatest commandment and the core of who we are and what the Christian faith is about.

While much can be said about loving God with all our thoughts, desires, and longings, let's focus on the call to love God with all our *strength*.

The word "strength" in this verse is packed with layers of meaning that a simple translation can't do justice to. *Ischys*, the Greek word used in this text, describes a forceful, active strength.

This isn't stiff-upper-lip strength, nor is it the strength of endurance we rely on and exercise through trials.

This is an actionable, aggressive strength.

What does this definition of strength stir up within you? How does it bring the passage to life?

According to this passage, we're to love God in such a way that we're on the offense and on the move. Our love should be rooting out and combating the things in our lives that prevent us from loving Him. Our love should take a hard look at our day-to-day as we ask ourselves, Do these things and plans actively love God?

Loving God with a forceful-strength love means taking a hard look at our calendars.

Our commitments.

Our goals.

Our hobbies.

Our planned rest.

Our free time.

Our already-filled-up time.

Our jobs, our bank accounts, our homes, our attitudes, our relationships.

It means looking at the things we say yes to and the things we say no to and asking ourselves, Does this reflect an active love for God? And if not, how can I combat complacency?

Perhaps loving God with all our strength means more family time and fewer seasonal athletics.

Perhaps loving God with all our strength means going to Bible study even when we feel tired or stretched too thin, because we recognize that making time for God is an act of love.

Perhaps loving God with all our strength means charting our screen time and asking ourselves how God might want that time to be used in a way that's more glorifying.

Write a few lines similar to those above, but tailor them for your life. What does loving God with all your strength mean for *your* day-to-day life?

Loving God with all our strength means fighting to keep Him the center of everything. It means putting every single decision in our lives (decisions made and yet to be made) before God and moving forward out of an abundance of love for Him and a desire to see His kingdom come.

Lord, take my life. Take my worldly, too-full, messed-up-priorities life and shake it up. Guide me as I exercise my strength in You and step into the kind of active love You want from me. And may that love pour out on others and reflect Your kingdom in a way that glorifies You.

Look at your calendar. Identify the commitments (yes, even the good commitments!) that don't reflect loving the Lord your God with forceful action. Are there one or two you could step away from in obedience as you practice loving the Lord your God with all your strength? Do that today as you ask Him to show you ways you can say yes to loving Him more.

ANTICIPATION FOR CHRISTMAS EVE

 In a seated position, close your eyes and place your hands palms up in your lap or at a desk. Take a few deep breaths with your hands open in a posture that represents being ready to receive. Allow your chest and belly to expand in all directions as you inhale. As you exhale, draw the area around your navel in toward your spine, assisting the exhalation of the breath.

Behold, the days are coming, declares the Lord, when I will make a new covenant with the house of Israel and the house of Judah, not like the covenant that I made with their fathers on the day when I took them by the hand to bring them out of the land of Egypt, my covenant that they broke, though I was their husband, declares the Lord. For this is the covenant that I will make with the house of Israel after those days, declares the Lord: I will put my law within them, and I will write it on their hearts. And I will be their God, and they shall be my people. And no longer shall each one teach his neighbor and each his brother, saying, "Know the Lord," for they shall all know me, from the least of them to the greatest, declares the Lord. For I will forgive their iniquity, and I will remember their sin no more.

Jeremiah 31:31–34 esv

Your Christmas Eve might be bustling with activity this year. Perhaps many friends and family will gather. Maybe you'll share a meal or two, and children will be begging to open gifts. Maybe you'll be working away in a hot kitchen or pulling people together to play some games. Perhaps it will all leave you exhausted—in a good way. In a way that comes when you're working hard for something that brings so much joy and beauty.

Or perhaps your Christmas Eve is going to be quiet and still. Perhaps there won't be a large gathering this year. Maybe you're spending it in a hospital or without someone you love. Maybe the kids are out of the house and spending the evening with in-laws. Maybe it looks different from how it was in the past, and that makes your heart sink.

Wherever you are tonight, whatever your gathering looks like—whether bustling and full or still and serene—remember this.

The baby Jesus was born. He lived and loved and died so the world could be fully reconciled to God. He gave His entire life for us—not only in death but in how He spent His time. In how He offered hope, peace, joy, love. All so that the world would one day be made right.

Imagine His return and all your longings satisfied and your burdens lifted in the blink of an eye. What does that stir in you?

Now imagine a brand-new earth for us to live and worship and work and do all of this on, in the way that was originally intended. Fully reconciled to God with direct access to Him and without the incredible burden of human brokenness. As you picture this restoration of humankind and all creation, what images come to mind? What feelings does this evoke?

We've spent these weeks of Advent reflecting on the hope we have in Jesus, the peace He offers, the joy only He can bring, and the love He offers to us forever. Have you experienced any shifts in your soul during this Advent journey?

Think about what you just wrote. Really let it sink in deep—and may you enter these days of Christmas and the New Year (and onward!) with more hope, peace, joy, and love.

Lord, Your desire to be with us in relationship is written all over the Bible story. What can I do now but choose to be in relationship with You? I choose to show up, Lord. I choose a life with You, a life of love. Help me to choose this each and every day.

Take a look back at some of the practices you engaged in during this time of Advent. Are there any you feel compelled to repeat or continue? Who in your life could support or join you in these? Write down which practices you'd love to sustain now and into the New Year, and share them with another person.

✦ Christmastime ✦

THE KING IS BORN

I mages and ideas of Christmas—mental heirlooms if you will—have been inherited and handed down over the years. And while many tangible heirlooms gather dust in lonely, forgotten attics, this collection of ideas about Christmas can adhere to us and affect how we cherish and celebrate the season. It can affect our emotions and experience of Christmas. This holiday is a good time to check in with our thoughts and feelings because it is filled with wonder and is, therefore, formative in our lives.

That wonder of Christmas is really because of the incarnation. Gifts and good food and gatherings come and go, but the wonder of Christmas that lasts is about God becoming human in Jesus.

Incarnation. That which is other, cosmic, mysterious, and holy became humble and human. God became newborn, fragile flesh and dwelled among us on this earth. What was difficult to grasp became skin-and-bone touchable. What was nearly impossible to see or define took on form. What all humanity was waiting for came. The abstract became embodied in Bethlehem. We call Him Jesus, Immanuel, God with us.

The entries in this part of the book are available to you if you want to step into the Christmas narrative in a meaningful and multisensory way during the season. The content we've provided for Advent is enough to take you right up to Christmas Eve and Christmas Day, but if you find that you long to engage the story as it's told mostly in Luke's gospel, this is here for you. The Scripture passages are longer to give more room for the detailed account Luke provided, but they aren't comprehensive. We don't explore every element of Jesus's birth, but the devotions invite you into the Christmas story in new ways. There are two entries for Christmas Day—morning and evening readings—and one for every day of the rest of the week, but use them however works well for you with the time you're given.

But do find some moments to be still and quiet, letting God speak to you and minister to you in a busy season. May this section offer an encounter with Jesus, which is as meaningful as Christmas gets.

INTIMATE AND COSMIC

A Devotion for Christmas Morning

Take a moment to intentionally pay attention to your immediate surroundings. Sit somewhere safe, feet flat on the floor, and close your eyes. Notice the ground beneath your feet. Notice the chair or couch supporting you. Slow your breathing. Be mindful of different parts of your body in the space around you. (Notice in the passage below that Mary says God has been "mindful" of her.)

And Mary said:

"My soul glorifies the Lord
    and my spirit rejoices in God my Savior,
for he has been mindful
    of the humble state of his servant.
From now on all generations will call me blessed,
    for the Mighty One has done great things for
        me—
    holy is his name.
His mercy extends to those who fear him,
    from generation to generation.
He has performed mighty deeds with his arm;
    he has scattered those who are proud in their
        inmost thoughts.
He has brought down rulers from their thrones,
    but has lifted up the humble.

He has filled the hungry with good things
but has sent the rich away empty."

Luke 1:46–53

The portion of Scripture we partake of this Christmas morning is called the Magnificat and has been famous in Christian tradition for centuries. The name Magnificat comes from the Latin translation of the word "glorifies" or "magnifies" in Luke 1:46. It's often sung in high church liturgy, and not just at Christmastime. Rightly so. Let's think about the context and meaning of Mary proclaiming this beautiful poem.

First, the context. It's hard to imagine all that was going on in Mary's heart in this season of her life. An angel had visited her with a message (earlier in Luke 1). This news was shocking and even scandalous. In an unbelievable nutshell: she would conceive by the Holy Spirit, outside of marriage, and give birth to the Son of God. Whether she was introverted or extroverted, she would've struggled to know what to say to people about this particular part of her life.

We don't know all her processing, but we do know she hurriedly went to visit her cousin Elizabeth and stayed with her for three months. It was just as well she left her village, with all the questions she'd be getting over the next months as her body changed shape around the Son of God. In the safe, comforting presence of a cousin and friend, and not in her hometown, Mary proclaimed poetry.

Have you ever gone through something that many people in your life couldn't understand? Was there at least one person who could relate and be present with you? What was that like?

Second, let's ponder the meaning of Mary's hymn. With everything going on inside her, we get to experience the bubbling up and overflowing of Mary's thoughts and feelings, even as Jesus grew as an embryo in her womb.

Mary shows us how to receive the news of Jesus in the most appropriate way: intimately *and* cosmically. Personally *and* globally. Individually *and* systemically. For our own heart and for the world.

What's something Mary declares this news to mean for herself? What's something she declares this news to mean for the world?

In the church, there's an ongoing tension. Our faith is absolutely personal. We have a personal relationship with the living Jesus Christ. *And* our faith is meant to be lived and practiced in togetherness as the church. Corporately, communally. That's what Jesus called His followers to—His first twelve followers and His subsequent followers, including us! Incredibly, at the very start of His life, on receiving the news, Mary proclaimed that Jesus came for her and for everyone.

Her joy over what this meant for her intimately was deeply attached to what it meant cosmically.

Jesus, to receive You fully is to receive You intimately in the deepest parts of my heart, where there's unbelief and fear and longing. Jesus, to receive You fully is to receive You cosmically, in this whole wide world, where there's systemic brokenness and pain. My soul glorifies, magnifies, You, God. You have remembered me today. You are the Mighty One. Holy is Your name.

Is there something you've been carrying alone that you don't need to? Is there something in your life that may be hard for everyone to relate to, but one or two friends could possibly or partially understand? Perhaps you could connect with them on this often busy yet meaningful day. Elizabeth didn't understand all that Mary was carrying. She was carrying God's Son! But she understood enough to give Mary the space and safety to release a lot of emotion (and theology!). Reach out to a friend today.

MADE FLESH

A Devotion for Christmas Evening

If you live with other people, go to their rooms and smell something that is theirs. Possibly smell a baby's blanket or spritz someone's fragrance or cologne. If you live alone or this seems difficult or too strange, try to remember your mother's smell or that of someone special to you. Do certain scents remind you of someone in your life? A certain food? A lotion? Or is there a scent that reminds you of past Christmas memories?

> In the beginning was the Word, and the Word was with God, and the Word was God. He was with God in the beginning. Through him all things were made; without him nothing was made that has been made. In him was life, and that life was the light of all mankind. The light shines in the darkness, and the darkness has not overcome it. . . .
>
> The Word became flesh and made his dwelling among us. We have seen his glory, the glory of the one and only Son, who came from the Father, full of grace and truth.
>
> John 1:1–5, 14

What a gift it is to have four very different gospel, or "good news," accounts of the life of Jesus. Matthew, Mark, Luke, and John. Luke's account has been the go-to Christmas story for centuries because he gives us details we crave: shepherds watching flocks, a bloodthirsty king, angels heard from on high, and a baby born in a stable. Matthew's gospel starts with Jesus's genealogy, showing that Jesus is a part of the line of the Jewish King David. He mentions information about wise men from the east following a star to locate the baby Jesus. Mark's gospel begins with Jesus already as an adult, with a voice calling in the wilderness, pointing back to the Old Testament prophet Isaiah. And the apostle John? His starts with some beautiful and theologically deep poetry.

John refers to Jesus as the Word, present at creation. What do you think that means? Take a moment to unpack that.

This passage is so meaningful. First, it tells us an important thing about the living God. God is a triune being—a being of three—made up of Father, Son, and Holy Spirit, who are all one within Himself. Second, this passage validates who Jesus was and is. Jesus isn't just a prophet or a king or a son of God. He *is* God, present at creation, creating as God. *"Through him all things were made"* (1:3). Third, this passage reveals to us that the way we can see God's Word—His heart and purposes and glory—is by looking at Jesus. God as a human being. In the four gospel accounts, we see who God is in the life, the death, and the resurrection of Jesus.

God's Word became human flesh in the person of Jesus.

What does it make you think or feel that of all the ways God could've shown Himself to us, to you, He chose to become human and make His "dwelling among us"?

Jesus is worthy of our awe and worship as the exact representation of God. But Jesus is worthy of our giving Him our whole life because He meets us *through* our lived experience. He's able to understand in a very flesh-and-blood sense what it's like to be human.

As you seek Jesus, which is hopefully what you're doing when you spend time with a devotional like this, remember who He really is. He's fully God, fully human. As you live this Christmas evening with Jesus, while you're celebrating and interacting with others, remember that God entered into the human story in a closer-than-close way in the person of Jesus.

There isn't one part of your human experience in the flesh that He doesn't want to do *with you.*

> *Jesus, You are the image of the invisible God. You came humbly, but You're high and lifted up. Of all the gods this world has worshiped over the millennia, none are like You, who chose to walk the earth as a human out of extreme love for us and in obedience to the Father. As I experience this world, I remember that You did too and did so fully human and fully holy. I want to live like You, Jesus. I want to be human like You are human. Amen.*

Pick one of the gospels: Matthew, Mark, Luke, or John. Schedule a time to read and absorb it—a day, a weekend, a month. Mark is the shortest gospel and can be read in an hour or two.

CURIOSITY VERSUS DOUBT

Pour yourself a glass of water. With how easily human beings can become dehydrated, you probably need it. Take a
moment and drink. Be revived. Receive even this simple gift from God.
He provided it. And science unequivocally supports that our bodies
need it. Think about how some of the things God offers and provides
for us can be harder to understand and even harder to swallow.

Then an angel of the Lord appeared to him, standing at the right side of the altar of incense. When
Zechariah saw him, he was startled and was gripped
with fear. But the angel said to him: "Do not be afraid,
Zechariah; your prayer has been heard. Your wife Elizabeth will bear you a son, and you are to call him John.
He will be a joy and delight to you, and many will
rejoice because of his birth, for he will be great in the
sight of the Lord. He is never to take wine or other
fermented drink, and he will be filled with the Holy
Spirit even before he is born. He will bring back many
of the people of Israel to the Lord their God. And he
will go on before the Lord, in the spirit and power of
Elijah, to turn the hearts of the parents to their children and the disobedient to the wisdom of the righteous—to make ready a people prepared for the Lord."

Zechariah asked the angel, "How can I be sure of
this? I am an old man and my wife is well along in
years."

The angel said to him, "I am Gabriel. I stand in the presence of God, and I have been sent to speak to you and to tell you this good news. And now you will be silent and not able to speak until the day this happens, because you did not believe my words, which will come true at their appointed time."

Luke 1:11–20

The story of Mary being visited by an angel while she was going about her day and the story of Zechariah's angelic visitation while he was fulfilling his duty as priest in the temple have similarities. It's easy to imagine the stories are set up in juxtaposition to one another. She's a young woman, probably doing tasks most women her age are doing that day in appropriate work wear. He's a male of a priestly line, with a specific role to play in the temple based on casting lots. He's in elaborate religious attire. They're both visited in an incredible way and given even more incredible news. They both respond with questions.

What's a story someone told you that was hard to believe was real? What's a truth about God you've struggled to believe is true?

Both these stories are helpful anecdotes because they show that asking questions of God isn't necessarily a sign of a hard heart. Life involves unanswered questions. Our God often invites us into circumstances before we know how they'll end, practically speaking. God knows us and loves us and understands us. He welcomes our concerns!

When is questioning merely curiosity and when is it unbelief?

Asking questions doesn't necessarily mean we have a heart of doubt. Mary asked, "How will this be . . . ?" (Luke 1:34). She was wide-open and soft with innocent curiosity. Zechariah asked, "How can I be sure of this?" He needed proof to believe. You can practically hear the heart of doubt and disbelief in his question. The angel Gabriel sounds incredulous in his response, as if to say, How dare a human being demand proof from a spiritual being who serves in the very presence of the living God? The angel doesn't give him proof. He offers Zechariah a second chance by means of a humbling process. One way or another, Zechariah was going to have to come to terms with his disbelief, either by walking into the unknowns of his life or through the creative humbling of not being able to speak for a time.

Even if nothing quite this extraordinary comes our way, we're given opportunities every day to hear and obey God without all the questions answered. We can ask questions—God can most certainly handle them—but can we also believe God for what remains unanswered? Being honest about our lack of belief increases our faith, but hard-hearted skepticism causes us to miss out on the power of God to do the impossible.

> *God, I give to You the unanswered questions in my*
> *life. When will _____ happen? How long will*
> *_____ go on? Will You meet the need of _____?*
> *Will the longing of _____ ever become a reality?*
> *How will You keep Your promises to me? Some of the*
> *promises of Scripture don't seem real to me sometimes.*
> *I believe, but help me in my unbelief. Keep my heart*
> *soft toward You even in the unknowns of my life.*

Be more honest than you've ever been before about what's hard for you to believe. In the presence of God, write down or journal some questions or promises or truths you struggle to believe. God can handle your honesty.

YES IN THE EXTRAORDINARY AND THE ORDINARY

 Do a short, simple household chore. Wash a couple dishes. Pick up some toys or clothes lying around. Take out the trash. As your body changes shape to do that task, notice what textures you touch, what makes contact with your skin. Notice the motion of your hands.

The angel went to her and said, "Greetings, you who are highly favored! The Lord is with you."

Mary was greatly troubled at his words and wondered what kind of greeting this might be. But the angel said to her, "Do not be afraid, Mary; you have found favor with God. You will conceive and give birth to a son, and you are to call him Jesus. He will be great and will be called the Son of the Most High. The Lord God will give him the throne of his father David, and he will reign over Jacob's descendants forever; his kingdom will never end."

"How will this be," Mary asked the angel, "since I am a virgin?"

The angel answered, "The Holy Spirit will come on you, and the power of the Most High will overshadow you. So the holy one to be born will be called the Son of God. Even Elizabeth your relative is going to have a child in her old age, and she who was said to be unable to conceive is in her sixth month. For no word from God will ever fail."

"I am the Lord's servant," Mary answered. "May your word to me be fulfilled." Then the angel left her.

Luke 1:28–38

Picture these scenarios. A long-awaited job offer. A positive pregnancy test. A diagnosis that immediately shifts how you think of your body. A friend moving away. A family member dying. Getting into a college after a few rejection letters. The timeline of our lives is forever changed, punctuated by these significant moments that mark the beginning and the end of seasons.

Can you think of a time when you heard some news that forever changed how you think of that room in your house or that activity you were doing? Can you picture it and even write down some words to describe it?

Mary probably never forgot where she was when she encountered the angel and received that news. Maybe she was getting water from a nearby well. Maybe she was preparing food in her home. Maybe she was sweeping aside dirt that had gathered. This young woman received a word from God that changed her life (not to mention history) forever. As unbelievable as the news was and as scandalous as the circumstances must've been, her response is stunning.

Has God ever asked you to do something that felt very difficult to say yes to because of all the unanswered questions?

Mary asks a question with a desire to understand better. Just one question. And the angel's response is almost humorously ambiguous. It *kind of* answers the question, but it leaves quite a few details out and raises even more questions. Ha!

What are a few questions you would've had for the angel Gabriel, if you use your imagination to put yourself in the shoes of a very young, unmarried Jewish woman two thousand years ago?

As central to God's story as her role was, it couldn't have been the role Mary imagined herself having in the story of the God of Abraham, Isaac, and Jacob. Her faith and God's favor are seen so vividly in her short response to the angel: "I am the Lord's servant. May your word to me be fulfilled." This is a striking response to God in prayer that we could borrow, but we mustn't forget that after she said this, the angel left. Mary held this heavy, explosive news in her heart *while* she went back to whatever she was doing before. Her life continued while she was waiting for the angel's word to be fulfilled. Her yes to God's unique calling on her life is remarkable, but her yes to continuing on with her life in faith that eventually the invisible would be made visible is perhaps even more remarkable.

God of Israel and of angels, this story is unbelievable, yet
I see within it an invitation to me. While my role isn't at
all like Mary's, I know You have something for me that

requires my faith and obedience. I long for a purpose that's pregnant with Your Spirit, O God. Sometimes it's hard to keep on with ordinary tasks when I long to see Your glory. Help me to be faithful and say yes to You in the ordinary things as I also pray, "Show me Your glory."

The next time you do the task you started with in today's touch exercise, pray a breath prayer: "I am a servant of the Lord. Let it be done to me." Repeat that phrase silently in your mind and heart as you inhale and exhale. Maybe place a reminder of this prayer close to where you do that task.

TIME AND PLACE

What was a national or global event that impacted you either directly or emotionally? Catalog the sounds of your life in that time and place. What were the background noises, the popular songs or soundtracks of that moment in history? If possible, do a simple YouTube search to see if some of these songs or sounds are available for a listen.

> In those days Caesar Augustus issued a decree that a census should be taken of the entire Roman world. (This was the first census that took place while Quirinius was governor of Syria.) And everyone went to their own town to register.
>
> So Joseph also went up from the town of Nazareth in Galilee to Judea, to Bethlehem the town of David, because he belonged to the house and line of David.
>
> Luke 2:1–4

On one hand, this passage of Scripture may not seem very significant. Perhaps these are just random details for the rare historian drawn to such matters. Perhaps, however, like the rest of God's Word, these words are there to give us a peek into precious realities available to us because of the hard work of these human writers who were filled with the Spirit of God. For the sake of today's entry, let's assume the latter.

Before Christ came, the years count back and we use the abbreviation BC or "before Christ." For example, 300 BC means three hundred years before Christ. Then Jesus came and we use *anno Domini* or AD, which means "in the year of our Lord." Although culture has shifted to use different abbreviations to accommodate those who don't identify with Christianity, without getting into technicalities let's just take a moment to remember that Jesus's coming marked a hinge in the world's history. "In those days . . ."

What marked the calendar, so to speak, on the date that Christ came, according to the Scripture passage? Imagine what could've been different had Jesus come a few months before or after that.

Ours is not a spirituality or a religion that's lofty and untouchable and floating and ethereal. Whatever historians or scientists or philosophers think of Christianity, the coming of Christ is written in history books. No one really debates the existence of Christ or the general events of His life. Jesus, and therefore Christianity, is tethered to a time and place, to flesh and blood. It's tethered to reality and humanity and history. While parts of faith or living for Jesus can feel subjective and hard to believe, the fact is that the incarnation took place at a specific time in history, in a specific town on planet Earth.

Why is it so hard for humans in general to connect faith in God with their daily life?

Do you ever find it difficult to connect the reality of God and the kingdom of Jesus with your daily life? How so?

The historicity of Jesus's birth should affirm the significance and spirituality of all parts of our life. The person of Jesus wasn't just long ago, and His coming isn't just someday. It's now. Jesus came to a specific now and for each of our specific nows.

God of the here and now, I remember in this moment that You sent Your Son Jesus to a time and a place. I experience the pull to make spirituality something detached, to make my following You something distanced from the day before me. This is the day You have made. You have creative works for me to do in partnership with You. I take a deep breath and realize that this very day, however mundane, is filled with Your presence. Thank You, Jesus, for choosing to enter into ordinary existence long ago and for continuing to break into my time and place with Your presence, for the good of the world around me and for Your glory.

What is an event on your calendar or to-do list (today or tomorrow, depending on what time of day you're engaging this entry) that you could infuse with the awareness of Christ? How would His coming, not as a baby but through His presence, change that activity or meeting or event?

FIGHT OR FLIGHT
OR FREEZE

Feel your pulse. You can find it on the thumb side of the inside of your wrist, to the side of your throat, or by placing your hand over the left side of your heart. Think about the last time you felt your heartbeat in your ear and head and throughout your body because your heart was pounding so strongly.

And there were shepherds living out in the fields nearby, keeping watch over their flocks at night. An angel of the Lord appeared to them, and the glory of the Lord shone around them, and they were terrified. But the angel said to them, "Do not be afraid. I bring you good news that will cause great joy for all the people. Today in the town of David a Savior has been born to you; he is the Messiah, the Lord. This will be a sign to you: You will find a baby wrapped in cloths and lying in a manger."

Suddenly a great company of the heavenly host appeared with the angel, praising God and saying,

"Glory to God in the highest heaven,
    and on earth peace to those on whom his favor
        rests."

Luke 2:8–14

In some ways, the characters of the Christmas narrative found in Scripture can be difficult to relate to. A teenage Jewish girl from a small village made pregnant by the Holy Spirit. An elderly priest confronted by an angelic being and then made mute. A group of sheepherders encountered in the middle of the night by an even bigger herd of angelic beings with a peculiar message. You get the idea. However, these very specific and uncommon stories are connected with very common human emotions.

When was the last time your heart quickened because you were nervous or afraid? What were you afraid of?

God seems to use fear to get the attention of many people in these chapters of Luke's gospel. He never wants them to stay afraid, and "fear not" is a common command given by God in the Scriptures. It's spoken over and over again to His people. God didn't create humans for fear and doesn't want us to maintain a state of fear, but undeniably fear is a by-product of the brokenness of the world, *and* He uses it to get our attention. Neurobiologically, when threatened our brain responds with fight, flight, or freeze. Many times in the Bible people experience this reflex before a life-altering encounter with the living God.

Is there a current fear God may be using to get your attention? Let's use fear as a loose term, anxiety or apprehension or dread being closely related.

The very things that elicited fear in the Christmas story were then used by God to reveal positive aspects of His character. Maybe we can be on the lookout for this same wonder in our own stories. Maybe we can look for how God is revealing Himself in the midst of our fear.

First, He might be revealing His glory, but never without His goodness. He doesn't want us to ever experience fear of His presence without the overwhelming awareness of His beauty and glory. Second, God uses creative means to provide peace. Usually peace doesn't come like magic, automatic and out of thin air. But God has been providing peace in the midst of fear throughout history. Lastly, these stories spread God's joy to those around us. The shepherds were given news that would bring joy for the world—meaning that they'd have to share it with others! Their fear would have to be overcome just enough to spread joy to the hurting world around them.

Lord of hosts, God of angel armies, You know all my fears and potential fears. You know what's giving me doubt and dread and apprehension. I take a moment to admit to You my fears. [Pause and pay attention to any fears you have.] Would You show me where You are in the midst of this situation? Would You show me Your glory? Just like the sky tore open, revealing the brilliance of angelic worship, would You break through my fears with the reality of good news of peace and joy for the world?

What's a story of peace and joy that came out of an experience of fear that you could share with another person today? Sharing stories can often share courage as well.

HOW WE HOLD WHAT HAPPENS TO US

 This may be easiest if you're at home, but feel free to do this while at the office or a coffee shop. Choose an object that has a bit of weight and hold it or carry it around with you for a few minutes. This could be a load of laundry, a set of weights, or a large book. Notice what that weight does to your body, your mind.

> When the angels had left them and gone into heaven, the shepherds said to one another, "Let's go to Bethlehem and see this thing that has happened, which the Lord has told us about."
>
> So they hurried off and found Mary and Joseph, and the baby, who was lying in the manger. When they had seen him, they spread the word concerning what had been told them about this child, and all who heard it were amazed at what the shepherds said to them. But Mary treasured up all these things and pondered them in her heart. The shepherds returned, glorifying and praising God for all the things they had heard and seen, which were just as they had been told.
>
> Luke 2:15–20

One of the defining characteristics of human beings is that we respond to things differently. Whatever the news, it acts as a presence, a weight that we must carry. We inevitably respond to what we hear and experience, and it's very hard to control these responses. Our personalities and past life experiences determine how we'll carry the weight of what happens to us. Isn't this in part what makes living with other people difficult? Our unexpected reactions to things often bring conflict because they clash with how others react to the same stimuli or trigger.

Can you think of a time recently when you responded to something in a way that was starkly different from those around you? How did you carry that news or experience? Try to use feeling words to describe it.

Jesus has always been someone who evokes a response. Even the announcement of His birth caused shepherds, kings, the young, and the old to react to the weight of it. We know King Herod responded to the rumors with psychopathic suspicion, wanting to find Jesus and kill Him. Wise men from the east went to great lengths to search out Jesus. An old woman and an old man, who had been longing for decades to see the Messiah, prophesied. And in Luke 2:15–20, we see that shepherds couldn't contain themselves. They found Jesus and spread the word, joy brimming over into news for all the world around them.

Yet Mary's response is a contrast to these. She'd literally been carrying the weight of it for months. And now?

"But Mary treasured up all these things and pondered them in her heart" (v. 19). What does this mean to you? Can you relate to this response? When have you treasured up something and pondered it in your heart?

Sometimes something holds so much meaning for us and elicits so many emotions that we can't easily express our feelings about it. It is too complex to invite others into that experience. Mary was the mother of Jesus, but she was also a human being, a female, a young person in a particular community with a particular role, and she had longings and dreams. The shocking news of Jesus was told to her, and the presence of Jesus literally grew inside of her for nine months until she gave birth to Him. Who could possibly understand what all she was feeling and thinking and experiencing in this unique role God gave her? Had she tried to share that with others?

In the undoubtedly lonely experience of carrying and birthing the Son of God, Mary found the best way to hold this knowledge was to keep it as close as her growing baby had been, deep inside, away from the evaluations and assumptions and judgments of others, and close to the heart of God.

What's an experience you can hold deeper and closer to God today?

God, You came to encounter our world through Your Son Jesus, and You continue to meet us in creation, in Your Word, and through Your church. As I move through my life, help me to have eyes to see You and ears to hear You. Some of the things I remember from my past or am experiencing now are too

much to carry in the presence of others, because they're either
too painful or too wonderful. You are near to me by Your
Holy Spirit. Today, I cherish some ideas and thoughts and
memories deep inside of me, close to You. You who can hold
any longing or experience I've had. Hold it with me now.

Whether you're an avid journaler or not, take a few minutes to write down something that happened to you recently or a long time ago that's hard to put into words, much less to share it with others. Try to write it down in words that are just for you and God. As you put pen to paper, remember God's presence and desire to hold your thoughts with you, even when you can't share them with anyone else.

MINOR ROLES

 Watch a five-minute clip of one of your favorite films. This should be fairly easy with streaming services and YouTube. Try to avoid watching the whole film instead of having this moment of quiet! Notice the characters in the clip and why they interest you.

Now there was a man in Jerusalem called Simeon, who was righteous and devout. He was waiting for the consolation of Israel, and the Holy Spirit was on him. It had been revealed to him by the Holy Spirit that he would not die before he had seen the Lord's Messiah. Moved by the Spirit, he went into the temple courts. When the parents brought in the child Jesus to do for him what the custom of the Law required, Simeon took him in his arms and praised God, saying:

"Sovereign Lord, as you have promised,
    you may now dismiss your servant in peace.
For my eyes have seen your salvation,
    which you have prepared in the sight of all na-
        tions:
a light for revelation to the Gentiles,
    and the glory of your people Israel."

The child's father and mother marveled at what was said about him. Then Simeon blessed them and said to Mary, his mother: "This child is destined to cause the falling and rising of many in Israel, and to be a sign that will be spoken against, so that the thoughts of many hearts will be revealed. And a sword will pierce your own soul too."

There was also a prophet, Anna, the daughter of Penuel, of the tribe of Asher. She was very old; she had lived with her husband seven years after her marriage, and then was a widow until she was eighty-four. She never left the temple but worshiped night and day, fasting and praying. Coming up to them at that very moment, she gave thanks to God and spoke about the child to all who were looking forward to the redemption of Jerusalem.

Luke 2:25–38

The films in our culture often have main characters and supporting characters. If you've ever watched the annual awards for television or film performances, you know this. Best male performance in a leading role. Best female performance in a leading role. Best male performance in a supporting role. You get the idea.

Do you ever feel like you have a leading or a supporting role in life? What feelings or thoughts does this question bring up for you?

This passage of Scripture is right in the middle of the Christmas narrative, between the shepherds and the wise men. We don't even know the names of the shepherds or wise men, but they seem to always be in the Christmas play. However, in Luke 2 we're presented with two people—who are mentioned by name!—and they're pretty important parts of the story. But they would definitely be more minor roles.

In the kingdom of God, lesser-known men and women are incredibly precious. Jesus demonstrated this in His actions to those He chose to spend time with. Even from the very start, His birth story includes those who would've gone unnoticed in society. These individuals were completely noticed by God, they heard from God, and they're forever remembered by God explicitly in the Scriptures. A man and a woman. Simeon, who was righteous and devout, with the Holy Spirit on him. Anna, a prophet, who worshiped night and day, praying and fasting.

Is it possible you're more seen and more a part of the story than you think and believe and act? How can you live today with more of an awareness of the significant and irreplaceable part you play?

God, the great Creator and Director of this story, I long for a significant role to play. Sometimes I feel like I'm nobody in this story of life. Sometimes I crave too central a role. You made me with the desire to belong and with a unique part to play. Would You put me in the right place at the right time and give me courage and humility to fill the role You have for me?

Look at the rest of your day. However busy or exciting or mundane, how can you enter into your unique role more fully and freely?

THE KING WILL REIGN

Instead of boxing away our intentionality and solitude and festive spirit with the Christmas decorations, we have an opportunity to continue to meet with Jesus and engage our senses into the new year. In many parts of the global church, themes of the Christmas story are pondered and celebrated into January. Specifically, if you study the timeline of the Christmas narrative, it's likely the wise men visited Jesus after the moment of His birth—perhaps even as late as His second birthday. As we continue to reflect on Jesus's coming among us both then and now, we hope the seven devotions in this section help prepare your heart, mind, and body for what God has for you next.

You may or may not be experiencing the sentiment of "Happy New Year." Maybe you're experiencing a surge of excitement as you develop resolutions and new goals. Maybe you're experiencing the dread of change or the pressure to perform better. Maybe you're craving newness as the year turns, yet life is pretty much going to be the same as it's been for the last five years. Or maybe you find yourself deep in the difficulties of life. Whatever your story, take a moment to envision the beauty of a fresh start.

While newness can bring apprehension or difficulty at times, it can also be refreshing and even God-appointed. Our craving for newness in our human lives can only be satisfied by the true newness that God initiates within our hearts. Preparing and planning, dreaming dreams, and resolving to change—these things are often good and right. But there's a newness that comes from the creative work of God. A newness that has nothing to do with our plans and resolutions and goals and abilities and everything to do with Him.

This newness is brought about by the Spirit of God. It's a fresh outpouring and breathing of life into us and our stories. It's the same newness that turned Paul's life upside down on the road to Damascus. The same newness that gave power to Jesus's followers at Pentecost. And the same newness that today urges ordinary people to gather together on Sundays, love their neighbors, and live the Beautiful Way. The truly best-laid plans are simple practices of obedience that lay bare our hearts to the life that Jesus brings. He wants to make us new (2 Corinthians 5:17). He wants to renew our minds (Romans 12:2). He wants to put a new heart in us (Ezekiel 36:26).

With that in mind, we ask, What newness does He have for you this new year?

YESTERDAY, TODAY, AND FOREVER

From your kitchen, your essential oil collection, or outside, choose a single scent from nature. Some ideas: a cinnamon stick from your spice rack, a sprig of mint from your herb garden, or freshly roasted coffee beans. Pause and inhale the fragrance. Take a long, slow inhale and exhale. Repeat three times.

> Jesus Christ is the same yesterday and today and forever!
>
> Hebrews 13:8 NET

The scent—whatever you chose to focus on today—is consistent. Cinnamon always smells like cinnamon, sweet and spicy. Mint smells like mint, bright and awakening. Coffee smells like coffee, earthy and rich. These scents are etched into our brains, powerfully so. We rely on their flavor. We don't think twice about throwing them into a dish or steeping them in water for a drink. We can identify them blindfolded.

Even with all the uncertainty of life, there are many things we count on and take for granted. The sun rising and setting. The seasons changing. Inanimate objects moving according to physics and chemistry. We count on our cars starting, our washing machines working, and, Lord help us, the automatic coffee maker turning on. We almost carelessly rely on these things happening. There's an underlying current of certainty even with the constant change of the world around us. We can be sure of the scent of cinnamon and mint, and we can be confident in the life-giving truth that King Jesus will never change.

Consider the way Jesus interacted with others in the Bible. Make a list of what characterizes Jesus's encounters with different people. (For reference, glance at any of the following: John 3, 5, and 8; Mark 2 and 7; Matthew 9 and 19.)

In the midst of a long letter full of instructions, suggestions, and explanations, the writer of Hebrews offers a profound and simple statement: Jesus does not and will not change. He's the same yesterday, today, and forever.

His extravagant love doesn't change. His gentle correction doesn't change. His careful attention to our lives doesn't change. His invitation to abundant life doesn't change.

Is there a change or event coming in the next calendar year that feels more doable when you remember Jesus's unchanging nature?

This banner, this declaration, should impact the way we live with Christ as King. We can live with bold confidence that the Jesus of the Bible is the same Jesus we serve. He doesn't fall victim to new revelation or our doubts and uncertainties. He's steadfast.

Lord Jesus, I'm surrounded by changes in the weather, in my body and my moods, in politics, and in the economy. You are steadfast. You are who You say You are, and You've been King since the creation of the world. I long for the day when the whole world changes, being made new, and You sit enthroned as King over it all. Hallelujah. Amen.

Read Matthew 5–7 while considering the truth that Jesus doesn't change. The things that were important to Him then are also important to Him now. How does this change the way you read that passage? How will it change the way you live today?

RISE WITH GOD

 Do a few neck stretches. Sit up nice and tall. Relax your shoulders away from your ears. Close your eyes. Take an inhale, and as you exhale, drop your chin to your chest. Inhale and bring your head back up. Exhale and drop your right ear toward your right shoulder, keeping your shoulders still and steady. Inhale and bring your head back to center, then exhale and drop your left ear toward your left shoulder. Inhale and bring your head back to center once more. Exhale and drop your chin down to your chest again. Now inhale and raise your chin to the sky slowly, carefully. Then exhale and bring your head back to center. Take a few breaths and notice how your neck feels. Repeat if possible.

> But you, LORD, are a shield around me,
>   my glory, the One who lifts my head high.
> I call out to the LORD,
>   and he answers me from his holy mountain.
>
> I lie down and sleep;
>   I wake again, because the LORD sustains me.
> I will not fear though tens of thousands
>   assail me on every side.
>
> Psalm 3:3–6

Inevitably, as we face a new year, we face difficulties and challenges. As we prepare for the year with our God, He longs for us to be honest about what we'll be truly facing. Real life isn't all exciting resolutions, fitness goals, and dreams.

Psalm 3 was written by David during one of the times he was fleeing for his life from an aggressive pursuer. He no doubt felt fear, betrayal, maybe loneliness. He says in an earlier verse, "How many rise up against me!" (v. 1). We may not have an enemy army after us or someone trying to assassinate us so they can have our throne, but we've experienced feelings that we're under attack or that people are against us.

What's something you're up against right now? Or you know you'll be up against this coming year?

The poetry in the Psalms is so helpful because it provides us with images we can keep with us. This passage talks about God being a shield around us. David used this metaphor because he'd certainly experienced the protection of a shield in his life as a warrior. This is speaking of physical protection and covering. But then David talks about God being our glory who lifts our head high. This is speaking to our honor and reputation. Even if everyone is against us, God is the one who protects that hidden part of us. We have no need to be ashamed. Because of God's provision to protect both our life and body and our reputation and identity, we can lie down and rest.

Where do you need God's protection now?

Does someone come to mind who really needs the Lord to shield them?

It's inevitable. We'll face opposition in our coming year, but even when something or someone rises against us, we can rest and rise again because of our protective Shield who lifts our head high.

God, I take this moment to give over my year to You with all its unknowns. Even tomorrow is full of unknowns. I can't shield myself from trouble, but I can stand firmly behind the shield of You. Help me to take each step with You, from the time I wake till I lie down to rest and all year long. Amen.

Write out Psalm 3 (the entire psalm isn't very long) on a card and place it next to your bed. May it be a reminder when you wake and when you lie down that you have a dependable and protective Shield about you.

EMPTIED HIMSELF

If possible, step outside and allow your skin to experience the elements. Only for a short amount of time, feel unprotected from the temperature—whether cold or warm. What does your skin feel like? What's the difference between the sensation of your skin that's exposed and your skin that's covered?

In your relationships with one another, have the same mindset as Christ Jesus:

Who, being in very nature God,
did not consider equality with God something to
be used to his own advantage;
rather, he made himself nothing
by taking the very nature of a servant,
being made in human likeness.
And being found in appearance as a man,
he humbled himself
by becoming obedient to death—
even death on a cross!

Therefore God exalted him to the highest place
and gave him the name that is above every name,
that at the name of Jesus every knee should bow,
in heaven and on earth and under the earth,
and every tongue acknowledge that Jesus Christ is
Lord,
to the glory of God the Father.

Philippians 2:5–11

It isn't possible in this short entry to explore all the depths and richness of theology in this passage. Volumes have been written on what it meant for God to become human—what He chose to give up, what He maintained. The wisest scholars only know in part. But today, let's take a deep breath and humbly remember that we don't have to understand it all. We can meditate on this passage as truth about God and His Son Jesus. Can we receive it in a fresh way today?

Where the passage above reads "he made himself nothing," other translations read that he "emptied himself" (v. 7 NET). Jesus as God's Son had every right and all the ability to shield Himself from the damage and dirt and danger that is the human experience, but He "did not consider equality with God something to be used to his own advantage" (v. 6). In other words, Jesus didn't value protecting Himself from a broken world! He didn't shield Himself from the elements of being human. His way of bringing restoration isn't to do it from a distance but to *enter into it Himself.* To enter by emptying.

When you think about Jesus, what are some things you know or believe from the Scriptures that He laid down or let go of in order to come as a human person?

When you think about Jesus, what are some things you know or believe from the Scriptures that He maintained when He became a human person?

Reading this passage, we can't help but picture Jesus as a naked, squirming, reaching, needing baby. His emptying involved becoming as fragile and needy a creature as one can be: a human infant.

During Advent and Christmas, we celebrated the coming of Jesus to our world as a baby, but now it's sobering to remember all that was ahead in life for that new child.

In your own words and from your memory, write down some of the events that were in the future for that newborn baby Jesus.

Jesus making Himself nothing didn't just involve becoming a fragile newborn, but it involved being a vulnerable man in the world, humbly suffering and being obedient unto death. A death that brought life to us. *His emptying brought us fullness of life!*

This time of year, we just spent weeks worshiping the coming King, but we're invited to demonstrate our response to Him all year long. As we enter into a new year, how can we be faithful to the vulnerable human life He lived? In this poetic, theologically rich description of Jesus by the apostle Paul, he says that the right response to Jesus is to imitate Him by descending ourselves. By emptying ourselves. By bowing before Him.

> *Lord Jesus, who entered our world in fragility and walked our earth with humility, who loved so fully, who gave Your life sacrificially, I worship You. I remember the years after Your birth as I enter a new year of my own life. I don't fully understand all You gave up. Will You soften my heart amid my questions and lack of understanding? Would You draw me to You in worship when the truth*

of You is too wonderful for me to grasp? This Scripture
declares so beautifully that there's no God like You.

Briefly bow in prayer every morning or night this week. We
don't have to bow to pray, and it isn't a part of our culture
to show respect with bowing, but the posture of our bodies
has the potential to affect our heart posture. Practice that
this week and pay attention to any shifts in your heart.

THE WHOLE WORLD IN HIS HANDS

Sing a chorus or two of "He's Got the Whole World in His Hands." If you don't know the song, you can find it with a simple YouTube search. There's a particularly joyful rendition by the African Children's Choir.

> For the LORD is a great God,
> a great king who is superior to all gods.
> The depths of the earth are in his hand,
> and the mountain peaks belong to him.
> The sea is his, for he made it.
> His hands formed the dry land.
> Come, let us bow down and worship.
> Let us kneel before the LORD, our Creator.
> For he is our God;
> we are the people of his pasture,
> the sheep he owns.
> Today, if only you would obey him.
>
> Psalm 95:3–7 NET

Some of us love and crave newness, getting energized and even euphoric with thoughts of a fresh start. Some of us get overwhelmed and stressed trying to plan for a perfect year ahead. And then some of us start out with the anticipation of failure, having been disappointed by too many fresh starts going bad way too early.

Are you a person who likes fresh starts? What does the new year usually bring for you in terms of feelings and plans? Is this a typical year, or do you feel different than in past years?

For all of us, the new year is the precipice of possibility. But God isn't watching us from far off, wondering if we'll come up with a plan that will please Him so we can succeed in becoming more likable to Him. No, He is near. He's with us as we gaze out over this precipice, whether it's out over a valley or a desert or a mountain range or a vast sea. Does it look filled with shadows and unexpected turns and forks in the road? Does it look dry and arid, without much provision or life? Does it look exciting and challenging with many much-anticipated vistas? Does it seem overwhelming and deep, like it just may swallow us whole?

Which landscape mentioned do you resonate with most as you "look out" over your coming year? How would you put words to your landscape?

Landscapes are vast. Our problems are vast. Our plans can seem vast. But nothing compares to the vastness that is God, who holds the world in His hands. Compared to His thoughts and His ways and His understanding and His power, we are like little children. Can we, in the presence of God, look out over the landscape of our year and declare with the faith of a little child that the days ahead aren't out of reach for our God?

Great God, I join the psalmist in kneeling as I declare to You: In Your hand are the depths of the earth. And I join the children in song: You've got the whole world in Your hands. As I look out over the year ahead, there are many things to be concerned about. Life is complicated. But I choose to bow before You and remember that You are mindful of Your creation. That nothing is too big or complicated for You. You care for me.

When what's on our minds seems so big and overwhelming, it's sometimes good to remember others and their particular struggles that are different from ours. Do a quick news search for an underdeveloped country and see some of the challenges that country is facing right now. Pause and pray for them.

A LONG LINE

 Look through a family photo album or scroll through family photos on your phone. If possible, find photos of extended family members or ancestors who have passed away. Notice how you feel as you take in their features and expressions.

> This is the genealogy of Jesus the Messiah the son of David, the son of Abraham:
>
> . . . and Jacob the father of Joseph, the husband of Mary, and Mary was the mother of Jesus who is called the Messiah.
>
> Thus there were fourteen generations in all from Abraham to David, fourteen from David to the exile to Babylon, and fourteen from the exile to the Messiah.
>
> Matthew 1:1, 16–17

Genealogies can bring an automatic skim mode to our brains when we're reading the Scriptures. In the Bible, wonderfully gripping narratives can be suddenly interrupted by a list of names we can't even pronounce. However, these factual lists can do more than provide information. They can remind us of our potential for change over time.

If we let our eyes linger on this list in Matthew and try to picture faces that represent stories, it can give a sense that Jesus's lineage was anchored in history and in human story. Jesus was a part of a long family line. (If you have the time, read all of the genealogy found in Matthew 1:1–17.)

When you think about your family line, what are some things you're proud of? What are some things you're not proud of?

It doesn't take long when reading the Old Testament to see that it's filled with disappointments, poor choices, scandal, pain, and disgrace. Even in Jesus's line, there are fissures and fractures that anyone would be ashamed of. It's so interesting that Matthew started his telling of the good news with this. Jesus was born into a family that was broken—and not any less broken than each of ours. In the genealogy we're even reminded of a famous story of infidelity and murder: "David was the father of Solomon, whose mother had been Uriah's wife" (v. 6). (It's a pretty scandalous story found in 2 Samuel 11–12.) The exile of Israel is also mentioned. Horribly wicked kings are listed. It's a spotty past.

If Jesus entered into a family and ancestry that was filled with pain and sin, what should that tell us about our families of origin? Are any reputations in a family out of reach of the redemption of God? Are any genetics out of reach of the redemption of God? Are any family habits or tendencies out of reach of the redemption of God? Jesus's family line answers a resounding "No!"

Not only are problems and mistakes a part of Jesus's own ancestry, but God had them included in the Scriptures. What we would possibly want to conceal out of shame, God had revealed and written down because it's a very real part of the brokenness of all families. *But it's never the last word.*

The brokenness of familial generations is never the last word in the beautiful family of God.

Remember, Jesus came to enter into the pain and reality of human experience. As you think about what's broken in your ancestral past and also in your family's living members, be aware that God is with you in your grief. But God also extends the invitation to make room in our imaginations for how He could bring redemption to our family. He makes room in our imaginations for how He could use *us* to bring redemption in our family.

If God knit us together in our mother's womb (Psalm 139:13), certainly He's intentional about the specific place and time we're born into our family line. Despite damaging mistakes and painful pasts, whoever is alive right now in your family could be His present means of redemption, changing the trajectory, disrupting that specific long line of human hurt. Maybe even starting with you.

> *God, in my imagination I stretch out my genealogy, my family line long in front of You. You know the names and faces and stories better than I do. You can see far back through the years and straight through layers of personality. In Your gentle presence, I remember things I wish I could forget, and I long for people who are no longer with me. Would You give me a way to see my place in my family line as a disruptor of patterns and breaker of chains? Even this coming year, help me to see myself as part of a new thing You are doing.*

What is a new way you can speak or act or live within your family of origin as you start this new year? Or the next time you're all together? How can you make a conscious choice to take a small step toward greater wholeness and life in your family?

SEEK HIS FACE

Put away some of your Christmas decorations, if you haven't already. If you have, look around at what was all decorated and festive only days ago. Remember the textures of those decorations. How does the room feel different? Draw, fold, or make a star to represent that the meaning of the recent season isn't over, even if the signs of it are.

> After Jesus was born in Bethlehem in Judea, in the time of King Herod, wise men from the East came to Jerusalem saying, "Where is the one who is born king of the Jews? For we saw his star when it rose and have come to worship him." . . .
>
> After listening to the king they left, and once again the star they saw when it rose led them until it stopped above the place where the child was. When they saw the star they shouted joyfully. As they came into the house and saw the child with Mary his mother, they bowed down and worshiped him. They opened their treasure boxes and gave him gifts of gold, frankincense, myrrh.
>
> Matthew 2:1–2, 9–11 NET

Despite what films and lift-the-flap board books would have us believe, the end of the Christmas story isn't when Jesus is in the manger. Nativity scenes and Christmas pageants tend to have a curtain call when the stable is full of animals, shepherds, angels, and wise men. But scholarship suggests it was most likely between forty days and two years after Jesus's birth when the wise men arrived! That's quite a range of uncertainty, but we do know this: Christmas Eve and Christmas Day came and went, and then the "three kings" took the stage. (The Bible never says specifically there were three wise men, although three gifts were specified.)

Wise men from the east are drawn to this King, but drawn differently than the others in the story. First, they aren't Jewish, and they aren't living in the Holy Land. They're probably pagan and know very little of the Torah and the God of Abraham, Isaac, and Jacob. Second, they're studying astronomy, and that's what God uses to draw them toward the Messiah and His place of birth. We know almost nothing about them, their background, or their journey; we just know they sought Jesus and they found Him.

How did God first draw you to Himself? What did that look like?

It's interesting that just when the Christmas story seems to be over and we put our decorations away, we have this part of the story that offers us a few important reminders. God draws people to Himself in different ways at different times. Angels appear to a shocking number of people in the Christmas story, but not to everyone. The wise men travel far and wide in search of a star as their sign of Jesus's location. Though it takes them awhile, they aren't late; they're right on time as they seek and then find the King of all Kings.

Maybe it isn't an accident that *after* the Christmas nativity scene we have this mysterious yet epic picture of what it means to seek Jesus: wise men from the east seeing His star and coming to bow down and worship Jesus.

What's helping you seek Jesus these days? How are you pursuing Him?

Christmas is over for now, but the seeking doesn't stop. The worship doesn't stop.

My King, I know You're calling me and drawing me to Yourself all year long. Even though I get distracted, even though I grow weary, I want to keep fervent in my searching after You. You aren't far from me, nor are You hidden. I don't have to decipher a map or scan the heavens to find You, but I want to be as zealous as the wise men in my pursuit! You say to seek Your face. Your face, O Lord, I will seek.

As you've thought through your coming year, have you considered who you'll seek Jesus with in the next season? Who are the people you live life with? How will you help them seek Jesus? How will they help you? If you haven't yet, take a step toward seeking Jesus with others in this new year.

CLOTHED WITH CHRIST

 Look through your closet and identify a favorite article of clothing. Maybe it's a fancy accessory that represents unique occasions and dressing up. Or perhaps it's your slouchiest cardigan for after work or your most comfortable hoodie for weekends. Put on this piece of clothing.

> The night is nearly over; the day is almost here. So let us put aside the deeds of darkness and put on the armor of light. Let us behave decently, as in the daytime, not in carousing and drunkenness, not in sexual immorality and debauchery, not in dissension and jealousy. Rather, clothe yourselves with the Lord Jesus Christ, and do not think about how to gratify the desires of the flesh.
>
> Romans 13:12–14

If we're honest, while the holidays are about gift giving and time with loved ones, we can also become pretty self-oriented. The ads and commercialism of our culture are purposefully geared toward us thinking about what we need (right now!) to be happy. Aside from this, our personal expectations of how the season should go can begin to be a burden we bear. Then we head into the new year with our resolutions and how we want to improve ourselves. If we aren't careful, we can slip into a total preoccupation with me, myself, and I.

Do you sense in yourself a need to shift away from thinking about yourself? No need to feel any shame about this. The mere realization is a step toward freedom and lightness. Just confess it here and move on.

The truth is that, as humans, we can't sustain self-preoccupation. We're created to think of others and be full of the awareness of God Himself. While we often run after things and people out of a desire to make ourselves happy, we know after a while that it's a wild-goose chase that leads to destruction, or at best leaves us dissatisfied. Full, abundant life means full awareness of God and Christlike affection for others. At this time of year, many of us experience a desire to be our fullest self, and we start clamoring for a better, truer identity. But the invitation to us is to put on Jesus, to take on His identity. That's the invitation—the identity of Jesus.

What's an identity you've been drawn toward that's a lesser identity than Christ's?

If we set aside for a moment our personal and possibly self-oriented needs and goals for the year, let's consider what a new year is really about. A new year begins another year of our salvation in Jesus and another year closer to King Jesus's return. It's good to be honest about our hopes and dreams for the year, especially if it can help reveal to us our longings. When they begin to take the form of a burden, we can lay those aside and remember what we absolutely need. The one thing we need to be complete and whole and satisfied isn't a gym membership, a spa day, or even a more vibrant social life. The world promises so much, but what we're made for is a true and deep identity in Jesus.

Jesus, in the safety of Your presence I invite You to show me where I've been preoccupied with myself and my desires. Open my eyes to what I'm taking on as my identity to try to make myself happy and feel good about me. Instead of wallowing in self-pity now, I turn to You. Yours is an abundant life and full identity that You mean to share with me. What wondrous love and kindness. Clothe me with Yourself, Jesus.

Inevitably, to put on Christ, we have to put off some other things. What is a practice or habit or behavior you feel Jesus gently inviting you to put off? This may be difficult and require changes, but it will probably mean greater lightness and freedom.

ACKNOWLEDGMENTS

I cherish the company of a particular cloud of female witnesses. The Mary Magdalenes, Perpetuas, Julians of Norwich, Corrie ten Booms, Lilias Trotters, Gladys Aylwards, Sojourner Truths, and Polly Willetts. This is an invisible but very real sense of belonging and courage for me whenever I go on a new journey.

Dear family and friends—your consistent presence and support serve as a trellis in my life.

Amanda, thank you for inviting me into this project and showing me the way. And for not freaking out (too much) when I thought I lost our manuscript.

Shalom, Sagesse, Moses, and Jubilee, I love you dearly. Life with you is exhausting and chaotic but rich and inspiring and hilarious. I LOVE how God made you and love seeing who you're becoming.

Anthony, I love our life together and the ways you give me a glimpse into God's love/*hesed* and desire to know/*yada* me.

Father, Son, and Holy Spirit, You are the ever-increasing love of my whole life. I want to go nowhere else except where You lead me, even into the driest of deserts.

—Hannah

Unending thanks to Hannah for journeying with me.

Thank you to Tad for always believing in me. To Roland, Zelda, and Brom for screaming and wrestling on the couch as I write this.

To Mom for being there.

To Chip for everything.

To Dana for praying for this book.

To the people of Northeast Christian Church, my community groups over the years, and the Monday morning women's group.

To Katara Patton for seeing the potential and Dawn Anderson for shepherding this book. To Joel for being so great and doing all the editorial heavy lifting for us, and everyone at Our Daily Bread Publishing for making this happen.

To you, reader.

And to Jesus, who doesn't just show up but is already here.

—Amanda

NOTES

1. Charles Scott Sherrington, *The Integrative Action of the Nervous System* (Cambridge: Cambridge University Press, 1906).
2. Bernice Ho, "The Mysterious Sixth Sense of Humans: Proprioception," *Scientific Harrovian* 5 (June 2020): 24.
3. Tish Harrison Warren, *Liturgy of the Ordinary: Sacred Practices in Everyday Life* (Downers Grove, IL: InterVarsity Press, 2016), 38–39.
4. Madhuleena Roy Chowdhury, "The Neuroscience of Gratitude and Effects on the Brain," PositivePsychology.com, April 9, 2019, https://positivepsychology.com/neuroscience-of-gratitude/.
5. Eugene Peterson, *As Kingfishers Catch Fire: A Conversation on the Ways of God Formed by the Words of God* (Colorado Springs, CO: WaterBrook, 2019), 80.

Spread the Word
by Doing One Thing.

- Give a copy of this book as a gift.
- Share the QR code link via your social media.
- Write a review of this book on your blog, favorite bookseller's website, or at ODB.org/store.
- Recommend this book to your church, small group, or book club.

Connect with us. [f] [○]

Our Daily Bread Publishing
PO Box 3566, Grand Rapids, MI 49501, USA
Email: books@odb.org

Love God. Love Others.

with  **Our Daily Bread.**

Your gift changes lives.

Connect with us. 🅕 📷

Our Daily Bread Publishing
PO Box 3566, Grand Rapids, MI 49501, USA
Email: books@odb.org